The Open University

A221 State, Economy and Nation in Nineteenth-Century Europe

Block 1: State

First published in 1995 by

The Open University
Walton Hall
Milton Keynes
United Kingdom
MK7 6AA

ISBN 0 7492 1158 X

Edited, designed and typeset by The Open University.

This book is a component of the Open University course A221 *State, Economy and Nation in Nineteenth-Century Europe*. Details of this and other Open University courses are available from the Central Enquiry Service, The Open University, PO Box 200, Walton Hall, Milton Keynes, MK7 6YZ, tel.: 01908 653078.

Printed and bound in the United Kingdom by Alden Press Ltd, Oxford

1.4

16316C/A221block1i1.4

Contents

Acknowledgements

Grateful acknowledgement is made to the following sources for permission to reproduce material in this block:

Unit 2

Figure 2: Gilbert, M. (1978), *Recent History Atlas* 1860–1960, 3rd edition, Routledge.

Unit 3

Text

Pintner, W. M. and Rowney, D. K. (1980), 'Officialdom and bureaucratization: conclusion', in Pintner, W. M. and Rowney, D. K. (eds), *Russian Officialdom: The Bureaucratization of Russian Society from the Seventeenth to the Twentieth Century*, The Macmillan Press Ltd, © 1980 The University of North Carolina Press; Pipes, R. (1974) *Russia Under the Old Regime*, Weidenfeld and Nicolson.

Table

Table 1: Wunder, B. (1986), *Geschichte der Bürokratie in Deutschland*, © Suhrkamp Verlag Frankfurt am Main 1986.

General introduction

Prepared for the course team by Richard Bessel and Clive Emsley

'In the beginning was Napoleon' (Nipperdey, 1983, p.11). This is the arresting opening of Thomas Nipperdey's massive history of nineteenth-century Germany. It offers a challenging way to begin this course – not simply as an assertion, but also as a question. Can we argue that nineteenth-century European history began with Napoleon?

On some levels, the answer clearly is 'yes'. Napoleon brought the ideologies, and legal structures of revolutionary France to much of Europe; Napoleon's military campaigns swept away old dynasties and the old order in large parts of the continent and gave rise to popular political and military mobilization which was quite new and modern; the post-Napoleon settlement, the Congress of Vienna of 1815, then fixed the political and dynastic frontiers of Europe for a generation.

In other words, if your focus is the political or military history of nineteenth-century Europe, then you might claim with some justification that 'In the beginning was Napoleon'. But could the same claim be sustained for an examination of the demographic history of nineteenth-century Europe? Certainly not! Another German historian, Hagen Schulze, in a book on Germany's *Path to a Nation State*, begins his background chapter (subtitled 'Europe's transformation from agrarian society to modern mass civilization') with the phrase: 'In the beginning was the demographic problem' (Schulze, 1985, p.49). He then proceeds to outline the explosive growth of Europe's population: from roughly 130 million inhabitants in 1750 to 185 million in 1800, 266 million in 1850, 401 million in 1900 and 485 million when the First World War broke out. This quite unprecedented development formed the context, as Schulze notes, for waves of migration and the gradual dissolution of old agrarian society which underlay nineteenth-century German and European history. This is not to claim that the demographic trends are somehow more important than the revolutionary changes brought about by Napoleon, or vice versa. It is to suggest, however, that there are different ways of approaching a historical period, and that many different changes and processes were operating simultaneously. The Europe which was turned upside down by first the French Revolution and then Napoleon was also a Europe whose population was growing extremely rapidly.

Similar observations may be made with respect to other approaches to the history of nineteenth-century Europe. It would be difficult to sustain a claim that Napoleon is the place to begin when examining the history of nineteenth-century European culture, or of gender relations in nineteenth-century Europe.

The same can be said with regard to economic history. The French wars had an impact on European economies, but you would have to examine long-term developments which owed little or nothing to the French Revolution or the spectacular military successes and failures of the world's most famous Corsican. The same may be said for a history which focuses upon the history of technology and technological innovation. Yet all these themes are important to an understanding of the history of nineteenth-century Europe; all affected Europe simultaneously; all involve different starting points, approaches and assumptions about how to order and assess our subject; and even though they are different kinds of history, they can and need to be interconnected. No historian of nineteenth-centry politics, for example, can ignore the attitudes towards population growth and shift. No historian of industrial development can ignore population growth and shift; and no historical demographer can ignore the impact of industrial development, urban growth, migration, increasing government activity, and so forth.

Matthew Anderson begins the set book for this course, *The Ascendancy of Europe 1815–1914*, with a statement which, while less dramatic than that of Nipperdey, is no less arresting when you consider its implications: 'The generation or more which separates the 1780s from the battle of Waterloo saw the beginnings of modern history in Europe' (Anderson, 1985, p.ix). The 'beginnings of modern history' no less – the beginnings of the history of the world which we inhabit! The basic assumptions with which we act in the public sphere (itself a modern idea) gained acceptance in the nineteenth century: that economic development is something dynamic rather than static or merely cyclical; that government should be for people, who should be represented in government; that society should be composed of citizens with equal rights rather than traditional orders with differential rights and obligations; that people have some national identity and that political organization should be coterminous with a national unit. Of course these assumptions had not met with universal acceptance by 1900 or 1914: Andalucian peasants hardly had tasted much dynamic economic development; the inhabitants of Prussia still had to contend with a three-class voting franchise; and the subjects of the Russian Tsar – not just Russians but Poles, Belorussians, Ukrainians, Jews, Lithuanians, Latvians, Estonians, etc. – were still a world away from a political system which recognized people as citizens with equal rights. But the assumptions had been placed firmly on the agenda.

The most profound assumption which gained acceptance in nineteenth-century Europe probably was a belief in progress. Note the title of Anderson's text: 'The *Ascendancy* of Europe'. Ascendancy over what? The nineteenth century was the century during which Europe came to dominate the world politically, militarily, culturally, economically and technologically. It was a century in which the lives of Europeans changed profoundly and, in many of the spheres which may be measured (e.g. mortality, income, education, housing), measurably improved – if not across the board, then certainly in large parts of the continent. So the metaphor which suggests a *rise* of Europe is not misplaced. Recently (at least in the multi-cultural United States, if less so in the EU-member-state which is the UK), the notion of Euro-centred history has been challenged; and there are good arguments to suggest that the history of the *twentieth* century has involved the unravelling of European dominance – a development which cannot be understood if we persist in purveying Euro-centred history. However, if one proposes to examine the history of the nineteenth century, which is the history of the formation of the modern world which we have inherited, then there are good grounds for Europe to be the focus and ascendancy to be the theme.

This, in very broad terms, frames our examination of nineteenth-century Europe, and explains why the aims we have set for this course are important.

Aims of the course
The aims of the course are:

1   to help you acquire some knowledge of the history of nineteenth-century Europe;

2   to give you an understanding of some of the historical debates concerning that history;

3   to assist you in forming your own, informed opinions about the processes of change in nineteenth-century Europe;

4   to enable you to develop some of the critical skills needed by the historian both in handling a variety of different source materials, and in communicating conclusions resulting from an analysis of those materials.

(You will also notice that dates are given in brackets after names of prominent figures. These are always, unless otherwise stated, dates of birth and death.)

On their own the aims are fairly bland if worthy statements. However, applied to the history of Europe in the nineteenth century, to a critical examination of 'the ascendancy of Europe', they can provide an exciting and exacting path towards understanding the world which we inhabit.

The course components

This course examines the history of nineteenth-century Europe by focusing on three broad themes: state, economy and nation. In each of these spheres, concepts and assumptions which frame how we view our world developed in Europe during the nineteenth century. We live in democracies, in which citizens expect to have equal rights before the law; yet the language of citizenship and the 'rights of man' was not spoken by many people before the late eighteenth and early ninetieth centuries. We live in developed industrial societies, in which there is an expectation of economic growth (or blame to be apportioned when that growth does not materialize); however, only since the nineteenth century have there been industrial societies and economies in which growth is considered a natural state, and this change occurred first in Europe. We live in nation states, and tend to consider this natural and normal; however, the European nation state (both in fact and as an ideological construct) is very much a nineteenth-century creation.

In order to explore these themes we have divided the course into three blocks, each of which focuses specifically on a theme and addresses a series of questions within it as follows.

Block 1: State

How and why did the nineteenth-century state develop as it did? What forms did it take? How did it define itself, manage itself, protect itself and its citizens?

Block 2: Economy

How and why did the economies of nineteenth-century Europe develop as they did? What were the contrasts between different economies both nationally and regionally? What were the respective roles of industrialization and commerce in economic development?

Block 3: Nation

What did 'nation' mean to people in nineteenth-century Europe? How, and by whom, was the concept used? Were there genuinely 'national' cultures, or were these essentially the creation of national governments and/or national enthusiasts?

The conclusion reviews the issues discussed in the course and examines the extent to which the Europe of the nineteenth century provided a framework for the Europe of the twentieth century.

Documents

A volume of documents is included with the teaching material. Historians develop their conclusions from studying primary sources. As you work through the blocks you will be required to study specific documents, to develop the technique of the historian in reading and analysing sources, and to extend your knowledge.

Set book

In addition to the teaching material there is one set book, M.S. Anderson, *The Ascendancy of Europe, 1815–1914*, 2nd edition, Longman, 1985. Like the course, this is not a blow by blow chronology of the nineteenth century in Europe. Each chapter explores a particular issue across the whole period. You will be directed to it continually as you work through the blocks.

Offprints

There is a collection of offprints. Here you will find articles and book chapters that we want you to read at particular points as you work through the teaching material.

Maps Booklet

Here you will find a number of maps relevant to certain developments in the period.

Audio-visual components

As well as the set book there are three 90-minute video-cassettes, four 50-minute television programmes, and two C60 audio-cassettes. The video- and audio-cassettes are fully integrated with the written text providing comment by historians of nineteenth-century Europe together with sources and images which you will be asked critically to assess. The television programmes focus on specific areas and issues, and develop in detail an aspect of the theme within the relevant block.

Doing History

One of our aims in the course is to enable you to develop the skills of the historian including the communication of your conclusions. That is a rather convoluted way of saying that we want to help you to write good history essays. Well, what is a good essay? As an example, let's take the introduction to your set book. On these three pages (pp.ix–xi), which at about 1300 words is just a bit shorter than we want from your TMAs, Anderson is setting the scene for his book. You could say that he was addressing the question: 'What was the significance of the period 1789–1815 for the history of Europe?' You will always be asked a question – which will *never* be 'Write everything you know about ...'. You should make sure that you address the question set, and do not simply 'write everything you know about ...'.

Exercise   Read Anderson's introduction (pp.ix–xi) now and note down:

1   how he has structured his answer (i.e. the theme of each paragraph and the overall direction of the piece);

2   whether you think it is following a chronological pattern? whether it is a chronology? and what the difference between the two is?

Discussion   1   The introduction has five paragraphs structured as follows:
(a)   stresses how little change there was in economies and social structures before the 1780s;
(b)   discusses the elements of change that were creeping in before the French Revolution; particularly with reference to government;
(c)   focuses on the change in the period generated by the British example of industrialization and parliamentary government, but more especially by the French Revolution and the ideas which it released;
(d)   briefly surveys the wars, and how they showed the potential of the new forces;
(e)   concludes noting much of Europe was still traditional in 1815, but it was struggling to come to terms with the new forces.

Overall it is a narrative of what Anderson considers to be the significant developments in Europe over the period and this leads on to the second point.

2   It follows a broadly chronological structure, beginning with the 1780s and working through to 1815. But, that said, it is not just a chronology – a list of dates and 'facts'. Good history balances narrative with analysis and interpretation and interweaves them. In this course we will be dealing with change through time, chronology thus becomes important. But we will also be dealing with the reasons for change, and this requires analysis and interpretation.

While Anderson is a very distinguished historian who has spent years researching, thinking and writing European history, his interpretations will not be universally accepted. Let us take a couple of examples of where what he writes might be challenged or at least nuanced.

On p.x Anderson writes 'Britain's wealth, her ability to sustain unflinchingly an unprecedentedly expensive and difficult struggle with France ... were a spectacular advertisement for industrialization and parliamentary struggle'. First the 'unflinchingly' might be challenged. It has, for example, been argued that the pressure of war, aggravated by, and itself aggravating, appalling harvests at the turn of the century brought Britain to the brink of revolution, and contributed significantly to the government signing the Peace of Amiens (Wells, 1983, and, to a lesser extent, Emsley, 1979). Again, in 1812 the British government was confronted with Luddite disorders in northern manufacturing districts, the assassination of a prime minister, and also by a massive campaign by both middle and working classes which compelled it to end the system by which it was engaged in an economic war with France. 'One does not like to own that we are forced to give way to our manufacturers' declared Lord Castlereagh, the Foreign Secretary (quoted in Emsley, 1979, p.160). So – 'unflinchingly'? A question might also be raised about the way Anderson suggests that British success provided an 'advertisement'. There were remarkably few in Europe who, after the defeat of Napoleon, considered the British parliamentary and industrial systems as models to emulate. Monarchs did not want to yield authority to chambers of peers and elected deputies – most of their seventeenth- and eighteenth-century predecessors had spent their reigns prizing power away from their nobles, and yielding power to elected representatives was what many of them had fought the French Revolution to avoid. As for industrialization, early nineteenth-century governments may have been impressed with developments in Britain, but were not sure how to follow, or indeed whether they wanted to follow such a route.

On p.xi Anderson concludes his comments on Napoleon: 'His own lack of moderation and statesmanship destroyed [his] power in 1812–14'. Yet there are those more sympathetic to Napoleon who would argue that the monarchs of Europe always regarded him as a *parvenu*, were never prepared to accept him as an equal, and were always ready to mount campaigns against him when they saw the opportunity. The distinguished

French historian of the revolutionary and Napoleonic period, Georges Lefebvre, believed:

> ... all of the powers shared in the desire to deprive France of her conquests, given the opportunity ... Europe's hostility is also explained by the aristocracy's intense hatred for Revolutionary France and for the parvenu. (Lefebvre, 1969, vol. i, p.302)

Others have emphasized fundamental weaknesses in the Napoleonic regime within France:

> ... Napoleonic power never succeeded in making itself secure ... when he ceased to win military victories Napoleon destroyed the only cement there was for national unity. (Bergeron, 1981, p.106)

Of course history depends on 'facts', but those facts have to be interpreted and communicated. Not every interpretation is valid or as adequate as the next and the conflict highlighted here between Anderson, Lefebvre and Bergeron is rather one of emphasis and focus; a longer piece on Napoleon by Anderson would, no doubt, take account of these other issues. What you have to recognize is that the moment any historian begins to explain why or how an event happened, he or she is interpreting evidence. But what is 'historical evidence'?

Historians draw their evidence from a variety of sources. On the one hand there are the texts of other historians – 'secondary sources'; on the other there is primary material – evidence created during the period being studied. The most obvious, and the most common primary sources used by historians are written documents. Anderson, together with the offprints and units for this course, constitute your secondary sources. We are also providing you with some primary material in your Documents Collection.

It is unlikely that a historian will ever find the 'answer' to the question which he or she is explaining in a single document. Evidence is built up from interrogating a variety of documents – and the word 'interrogating' is used here advisedly. Of course you have to understand the information deliberately and openly expressed in a source, but you also have to think about the assumptions which are behind it; what is not explicitly stated can be of considerable significance.

Exercise   On p.x Anderson stresses the importance of the Declaration of the Rights of Man and Citizen which was adopted by the French National Assembly on 26 August 1789. The first three clauses of the Declaration read as follows:

1   Men are born and remain free and equal in rights. Social distinctions may be based only on common utility.

2   The aim of all political association is to preserve the natural and imprescriptable rights of man. These rights are liberty, property, security, and resistance to oppression.

3   The principle of all sovereignty rests essentially in the nation. No body and no individual may exercise authority which does not emanate from the nation expressly.

(Quoted in Lefebvre, 1947, p.189)

Given what Anderson tells you about governments in the late eighteenth century in his first two paragraphs, what does this document say about the forms of government existing in the eighteenth century and why should this have posed a threat to the established systems of government and authority?

Discussion   Well, the three clauses quoted above say nothing explicitly about the eighteenth-century systems of government, but the implications of what they do say run counter to those systems of government. At the close of his opening paragraph Anderson describes a society based on traditional orders with different legal rights. The Declaration of the Rights of Man and Citizen states, at the outset, that all men are equal in rights and then goes on to declare that the aim of political association is to preserve these rights. Anderson describes the governments of Europe as, mainly, absolutist monarchies. Increasingly these liked to think of themselves as working for their subjects. The Declaration, however, proclaims that sovereignty rests in the nation, and that only the nation can give authority to rulers. It also, significantly, declares the 'rights' it is describing to be those of 'man' and 'citizen'; the idea of 'man' as 'subject' (and remember that the people of monarchs are commonly described as 'subjects' (*sujet* in French, *Untertan* in German)) was not in the minds of the men who drafted the Declaration.

A few other points might also be made about the ideas underlying the Declaration which we would not expect you to have grasped, but which a deeper knowledge of the period can help to draw out. First it can justifiably be argued that when they used the term 'man' (*homme*) the National Assembly really were discounting women. At the same time probably some were also discounting men without property; initially during the French Revolution a distinction was made between active and passive citizens – only the former, men who were over 25 and who paid the equivalent of three days unskilled labour in taxes, were given the right to vote. War, and the need to deploy all of the nation's young men on the battlefield, helped bring an end to this distinction in 1792, though subsequent regimes re-established voting qualifications.

Finally, it is worth noting the use of 'nation' in the Declaration. 'Nation' was not a new word, but it did acquire new levels of meaning with the Revolution. The old regime was characterized by the motto '*Un roi, une foi, une loi*' ('one king, one faith, one law'), but this was replaced in 1789 by '*La Nation, la loi, le roi*' ('the Nation, the law, the king') and with the fall of the monarchy in 1792 the 'nation' became even more plainly central.

Nation is one of the key words in this course. It is important to grasp that it, like 'economy' and perhaps especially 'state' as well as other important words, has different meanings. Such meanings have developed over time. You need to be clear about the different ways in which particular words are used, and when you meet or use these words yourself you must be absolutely clear which of the meanings is intended. But please, this does *not* mean that when you start an essay you have to spend several hundred words defining your terms. Common sense, care and thought will see you through.

Summing up

This introduction has been kept deliberately short, and limited largely to presenting themes and questions which will be discussed in the course and which you will have to address as you work through the course materials. These themes and questions will, we hope, help provide some threads to help you organize your path through the course. As with any history course, there is a lot of information which you will need to digest: changing borders, the backgrounds and positions of political figures, structures of government, the course of political and military campaigns, evidence of economic development, and – it must be said – names and dates. All this may make little sense, and probably will be impossible to remember, without the signposts which the overarching themes and questions offer – without reasons for needing to know, for example, what states emerged from the Congress of Vienna, or how and when the French government bureaucracy developed, or who were Giuseppe Mazzini (1805–72), Prince Alfred von Windischgrätz, or Count Sergei Witte. In order to make the best use of the course materials, you will need to keep the overarching themes and questions in focus.

By the same token, however, it will be difficult to assess these themes and questions without having a good grasp of the framework of nineteenth-century European history. It is to this which we now turn. Indeed, the real work associated with this introduction begins now: reading the set book. M.S. Anderson's *The Ascendancy of Europe 1815–1914* was chosen because it offers a good clear outline of the history of nineteenth-century Europe.

Please read through *The Ascendancy of Europe 1815–1914* now, keeping in mind the broad themes discussed above and noting any points which may puzzle you. At this point you should not try to master detail – just aim to get the broad sweep of the period. You might find it useful to take notes – but not detailed notes. It will probably be best just to jot down the general argument at the end of each chapter. You will be re-reading most of the book in detail with the different blocks of the course materials.

References

Anderson, M.S. (1992), *The Ascendancy of Europe 1815-1914*, 2nd edn, Longman, London.

Bergeron, L. (1981), *France under Napoleon*, Princeton University Press, Princeton N.J.

Emsley, C. (1979), *British Society and the French Wars 1793–1815*, Macmillan, London.

Lefebvre, G. (1947), *The Coming of the French Revolution*, Princeton University Press, Princeton N.J.

Lefebvre, G. (1969), *Napoleon*, 2 vols. Routledge and Kegan Paul, London.

Nipperdey, T. (1983), *Deutsche Geschichte 1800–1866. Bürgewelt und starker Staat*, Beck, Munich.

Schulze, H. (1985), *Der Weg zum Nationalstaat. Die deutsche Nationalbewegung. 18. Jahrhundert bis zur Reichsgründung*, Deutscher Taschenburch Verlag, Munich.

Wells, R. (1983), *Insurrection: The British Experience 1795–1803*, Alan Sutton, Gloucester.

Unit 1
Introduction

Prepared for the course team by
Clive Emsley

Study timetable

Weeks of study	Texts	Video	AC
2	Unit 1, Offprint 1	Video 1	

It should also be noted that TV1 and TV4 are of interest to the study of this unit.

This first block in the course looks at the nineteenth-century European state: what it was, how it developed, the differences and similarities between its various manifestations. In working through this brief introduction you will need to refer to material in your Offprints and to Video 1. Given the problems of TV scheduling it is impossible to note at what precise point TV1, 'A Tale of Two Capitals: Paris and Rome' will be broadcast. It has, however, been prepared with specific reference to the content of this block and addresses the way in which two capital cities developed during the nineteenth century in relation to their respective states. TV4, 'Changes in Rural Society: Piedmont and Sicily', is also relevant since, among other things, it addresses the impact of the state upon the country people of two very different regions of nineteenth-century Italy.

Well, what is a state? What is a nation-state? We all live in one, so we all ought to know. But when we get down to trying to spell matters out precisely, things get a bit difficult. In general terms, is a 'state' a country? Are its inhabitants automatically included when we talk for example, about 'the state going to war'? Who made the decisions about the state going to war, or providing welfare and education, or raising taxes? Is the state rather a set of institutions and the people who run it? Is the state a two-way relationship in which the inhabitants are expected to fulfil certain obligations, and the government and administration reciprocate? Maps 1 and 3 in the Offprints Collection (pp.1 and 3) show Europe roughly at the beginning and end of our period. These show the borders of the states with which we are dealing. You will probably find it useful to refer to these maps throughout the course. But I want to start with a short exercise using graphics which you will find in Video 1, section 1, and which runs on from the brief introduction to the video.

Video Exercise
Watch Video 1, section 1 now. (I am not setting you any specific task here other than watching the first section of the video – watching it will, I hope, focus some of the issues about the boundaries of nineteenth-century states and (for future reference) the creation of nation-states.)

The history shelves of our bookshops and libraries are full of books on states/nation-states. Many, perhaps most, take modern frontiers more or less for granted, and then proceed to explain, with varying emphases and over varying periods, how states were formed and developed, in whose interest, their military and diplomatic triumphs and disasters, their economic and social developments. 'State' here can be interchangeable with 'country' 'power', even 'nation', and, perhaps also, 'government'. The social-science shelves in the same bookshops and libraries have other books on the 'state' or 'states', sometimes with a historical perspective, but generally rather more concerned with attributes, definitions, and structures. A recent social-science text has concluded that:

> There is a great deal of agreement amongst social scientists as to how the state should be defined. A composite definition would include three elements. First, the state is a set of institutions; these are manned by the states own personnel. The state's most important

institution is that of the means of violence and coercion. Second, these institutions are at the centre of a geographically-bounded territory, usually referred to as a society.

Crucially, the state looks inwards to its national society and outwards to larger societies in which it must make its way; its behaviour in one area can often only be explained by its activities in the other. Third, the state monopolizes rule making within its territory. This tends towards the creation of a common political culture shared by all citizens. (Hall and Ikenbury, 1989, pp.1–2)

Now the authors are careful to say 'a great deal of agreement'; they are also careful to go on, in a later paragraph, to list a string of exceptions to, and problems with, their definition. Furthermore, a difference of approach, a different historical tradition, can lead to very different emphases. The first question which we posed to the historians interviewed for Video 1 asked them for their definition of the nineteenth-century state. In replying they spoke at length in a sophisticated way – academics tend to hedge and qualify and expand when they give definitions.

Video Exercise   Watch Video 1, section 2, now and briefly note down the differences and
                     similarities in the way that Professors John Breuilly, Wolfgang Mommsen
                     and Jean Tulard approached the state – and let me emphasize the *briefly*,
                     don't attempt to copy out what they say word for word, these were off-the-
                     cuff responses to questions, not long thought-through and carefully pre-
                     pared answers. Remember, while they were aware that this was for an
                     introductory student video, they made no concessions. This is tough stuff,
                     and more complex than you will find in subsequent units. If you find it very
                     difficult read my short discussion *alongside* their comments. Above all
                     don't be afraid of it and don't think that you have to *learn* everything that
                     is said. What you need to do is to *understand* the gist of what is being said.

Discussion   There is agreement that the state is abstract. John Breuilly suggests
                     that different historical experiences have contributed to different percep-
                     tions of the state. Thus the major political changes in nineteenth-century
                     France and Germany necessitated a more abstract perception to under-
                     stand any continuity. In Britain, in contrast, nineteenth-century political
                     struggles were about the franchise rather than the form of the government
                     and people tend to think more in terms of 'government' and 'parliament'
                     rather than 'state'. Jean Tulard emphasizes the differences he perceives
                     between the state and the nation (another abstract concept, but we will be
                     looking at that in Block 3). The former, he argues, is a political structure
                     which, can, and does change; nation, however (and here it is tempting to
                     suggest that, as a historian of the revolutionary and Napoleonic period,
                     Tulard has absorbed some of the romantic enthusiasm of these years), is
                     homeland, 'feeling', 'a glass of wine' – Professor Tulard can get away with
                     it, but you are advised to be a little more concrete in your TMAs and exam
                     answers.

                     Wolfgang Mommsen considers that the continental view of the state is
                     rather different from that held in Britain; it includes elements that the
                     British would encompass in the word 'society'.

There is no reason why, in your essays, you cannot still use 'state' interchangeably with words like 'power' and 'country', we are not intending to be prescriptive about definitions and usage. But make sure it is clear what you mean, and remember that it is the 'state' in Hall and Ikenbury's social-science sense with which we are primarily concerned in this block.

States in this sense existed, or were at least developing, long before the nineteenth century. Generally they centred on a successful dynasty or other structure (a city-state, theocracy etc.) which showed an ability to raise taxes and survive wars – the two were invariably linked. But the nineteenth century witnessed significant developments in several key areas.

I want you now to turn to Offprint 1. You may not find this a particularly easy piece. Poggi notes early on that he is using 'a high level of abstraction'. He also points out that he is ignoring considerable differences in constitutional structures; and he makes references to a number of theorists many of whom may mean little or nothing to you. Don't worry about this. The idea is to get a grasp of what Poggi thinks was new and significant about the European state in the nineteenth century – he is, here, drawing attention to *specific* nineteenth-century features in contrast to those discussed in earlier chapters of his book about other kinds of state. Try to be critical; but don't worry if you cannot challenge any of Poggi's ideas or interpretation – you are, after all, only just beginning the course.

Exercise   Read Offprint 1 now. Try briefly to summarize the developments which Poggi discusses; try also to note his own attitude to the state system and the way in which he believes states, and their inhabitants, relate towards each other.

Discussion   Poggi notes the following as common elements to the nineteenth-century constitutional state.

1   Each was a self-originating, self-empowered unit operating in its own interest.

2   Each claimed sovereignty in its own territory, with a unitary system of law, finance (and as far as possible), language. (There could be problems for this unity with developing rivalries between different instruments of government, and with one section of the citizenship – the haves – being favoured and protected by the system.)

3   Each appears to have been consciously built. There are notions of states functioning as machines, but in reality they contain elements of both traditional, face-to-face communities (*Gemeinschaft*) and impersonal associations (*Gesellschaft*).

4   Each functioned through law, and law specified the rights and duties of citizens. (State apologists had problems in explaining how the state could be subservient to the law.)

5   Each experienced the growth of 'civility', of parliaments, and of various groups participating in the political process.

6   Each experienced a similar clutch of political issues – how the state should be governed; what its relationship with its peers should be; how to deal with the 'social question' and 'economic management'.

Poggi's view of the world has elements that some political scientists classify as the Realist Perspective. He perceives the state as greedy and selfish; there is no real order in the state system, rather each is out for itself. If there was no major international war between 1815 and 1914, this was less because of the international management systems which had evolved, and more because (a) hostilities were relegated to the parts of the world being exploited by the European states; (b) the increasingly dominant European bourgeoisie recognized that peace was in its interest; and (c) the memory of the terrible bloodletting of 1792–1815.

There is also, you may think, a Marxist tone to the way Poggi describes some of the potential for friction within the unitary states – time and again he stresses the development of class struggle. There are, of course, alternative approaches. If major international war was so rare among the nineteenth-century states of Europe, might it not have been because there was a balance between them; that statesmen seriously believed that they were living in a progressive age, and that war should be the last resort – and after all, isn't it, in the end, men who make war, not impersonal entities? Why should the relations between states be character-ized principally by free-for-all competition and the survival of the fittest?

Video Exercise   Watch Video 1, section 3 and note briefly how far the comments of Profes-sors Eric Hobsbawm, Mommsen, Breuilly and Paul Preston fit with Poggi's overview.

Discussion   There is broad agreement with Poggi here. Hobsbawm, for example, stresses the increasing capability of the state in securing its public order through police systems, reaching and integrating its furthest villages with a postal service, monitoring and educating its citizens. But I hope that you noted how each contributor had a different emphasis. Mommsen, for exam-ple, describes an expanding system of rational administration seeking to take increasing responsibility over welfare, education and economic development. A professional bureaucracy emerged to run the administra-tion. There was a general expansion of political systems to incorporate more and more of the population; this generally resulted in friction, though in different degrees – in Britain it was less acute than in Italy or Germany. Breuilly emphasizes the significance of Liberalism and the way in which it divided spheres of activity – religion and the economy for example, but with the state claiming a monopoly in the sphere of politics.

But historians must be able to separate the particular – of course every state had its particularities and peculiarities. Spain, in Paul Preston's description, appears rather different from the general pattern – an old, largely feudal state, seeking to hang on to its position as an imperial power, not particularly interested in forging anything new, but in making work what it had.

Whether or not we, as individuals, agree with Poggi's way of approaching the modern European state system we can accept the changes which he describes as a starting point, if not equally applicable to each and every state. Many of the points he makes are familiar, and he discusses things which we now tend to take as typical, indeed natural, components of the states in which we live.

Linking Poggi with the quotation from Hall and Ikenberry (pp.3–4, above) we might say that there are three basic aspects to the state:

1   its internal features as an institutional apparatus;

2   the relations between that apparatus and the society which the apparatus controls/serves;

3   the external relations between states.

This block focuses on elements of the first two aspects exploring constitutions and welfare (the second aspect) and bureaucracy and legitimate force (the first aspect).

1   During the nineteenth century **constitutions** began to be introduced outlining government structures and the rights and duties of citizens.

2   Substantial and sophisticated **bureaucracies** were established to run these states – to raise taxes and armies, and to supervise quite new areas of government concern, such as education and welfare.

3   The states claimed the sole right of **legitimate force** within their territories, and the growing bureaucracies included new police forces whose tasks included the protection of the inhabitants from crime and disorder, and the protection of the government and its administration (the 'state', if you like) from angry and/or disaffected inhabitants.

4   The bureaucracies also began to develop policies for the **welfare** of a state's inhabitants.

Remember throughout, however, the importance of contingency and different national experiences. To rehearse some of the ideas that we have already discussed, and to raise some new questions about the issues in this block, I now want to set you some exercises out of the material on the remaining three sections of Video 1.

Video Exercise   History involves interpreting sources, but interpretation might depend on the questions that the historian asks of a document and the manner in which he or she approaches it. In the general introduction to the course I touched on the significance of the Declaration of the Rights of Man and Citizen. Watch Video 1, section 4, and note down the different approaches to the significance of that document taken by Jean Tulard and Hazel Mills.

Discussion   Tulard stresses the way in which the revolutionaries rapidly put down a few basic principles at the beginning of the Revolution when its future was uncertain. It is interesting too, how he stresses the pre-eminence of the French language at the end of the eighteenth century which probably underlined, for those revolutionaries, their belief that they were constructing something for all Europeans. Mills puts her emphasis on the gender orientation of the document, noting that even the most radical government of the Revolution maintained the gender bar in its perception of citizenship.

Of course, one of these interpretations is not right and the other wrong; both are based on considerable knowledge. Tulard and Mills are approaching the document from different angles and formulating different perceptions of its significance. It would be difficult also to accuse either, or both, of them as being insufficiently objective. Tulard is a historian of the politics of the revolutionary and Napoleonic period, and I think it is fair to say that he takes a pride in the promise of the document; Mills's research has concentrated on women and welfare in nineteenth-century France, and her discussion is filtered through her perception of the position of those women.

Video Exercise   The growth of the state during the nineteenth century led to the growth of state bureaucracies and in theory this meant that trained professionals, acting with even-handedness and probity, replaced an older system, which we would call cliental, and in which individuals rendered and sought favours and put family, friends or social groups first. But if states differ, what about their bureaucracies? And how can we account for these differences? Watch Video 1, section 5, which presents comments from Paul Preston, Paul Ginsborg, Edward Acton and David Englander; note down the differences stressed here, and the reasons for those differences.

Discussion   Preston and Ginsborg, respectively historians of Spain and Italy, both argue that, by the end of the nineteenth century at least, there was a significant difference between the bureaucracies of northern and southern Europe. Preston stresses that there was virtually no political change in either country, that participation in the political process was confined to the few who were intent on using the system to maintain their authority. Spain had an army of pen-pushers, but no professional bureaucracy. For Ginsborg the problems in Italy arose out of the state's failure to eliminate clientage and impose its own rules of equity, efficiency and transparency; indeed, he argues, the state itself became engulfed in clientage and that the problem has continued throughout the twentieth century.

But before we come to think in simple terms of a corrupt southern Europe and upright, incorruptible bureaucrats in the north, remember Edward Acton's discussion of the situation in Russia where, in the early part of the nineteenth century, an all-powerful Tsar often felt frustrated by the lack of information that he received from his small, corrupt administration, and where, even in spite of significant efforts by a group of efficient jurists from the middle of the century, the bureaucracy continued to be dominated by a conservative gentry. Furthermore, even where a bureaucracy may have approached levels of probity, as in Britain, as David Englander explains, there could be considerable resistance to reform and here Oxbridge had the examination system sewn up while key sections of the civil service (the Foreign, Scottish and Irish Offices) all succeeded in being exempted from the regulations emanating from the Northcote–Trevelyan reforms.

One of the areas in which these bureaucrats worked was the administration of state welfare. We have already noted how nineteenth-century states began to take responsibility for the welfare of their citizens, but we have not asked the question why they did this and was there no welfare before. Video 1, section 6 addresses these questions.

Video Exercise

Watch Video 1, section 6 now and note down the suggestions as to why the state became involved in welfare, and who else was involved. We might tend to assume of welfare provision as a part of progress, and this is how it has often been described, especially in the British context. But was it that simple? Did rulers act through altruism? Did they have other agendas? What other social groups encouraged what we can call 'social action', and how did they continue to be even as the nineteenth-century state expanded?

Discussion

Englander suggests that there are two extremes of interpretation of the development of welfare in the nineteenth century. At one pole there is the insistence that the recognition of social need was progressive and humanitarian (something which appeared to fit well with the British experience); at the other is the suggestion that welfare was introduced to integrate potentially subversive elements at the time when international rivalries were increasing. Both Englander and Mills stress the role of Christianity (in general) and the Church as an institution in carrying out welfare tasks but also in making governments aware of social problems. Hazel Mills warns that, perhaps, too much stress has been put on the clash between church and state in the nineteenth century (though remember that states were increasingly jealous of their power and authority).

Much welfare, especially for the first two-thirds of the century, remained outside the state's remit. It was one of the few areas in which women could perform a public role.

All of these issues will recur in the block which follows – many will recur throughout the course. At the end of this block you should have an understanding of major developments in the nineteenth-century European state and be able to offer some explanation for the differences between different countries.

References

Hall, J. A. and Ikenberry, G. J. (1989), *The State*, Open University Press, Milton Keynes.

Unit 2
States and constitutions

Prepared for the course team by Clive Emsley

Contents

Study timetable

Weeks of study	Texts	Video	AC
2	Unit 2; Documents I.1–I.13	Video 1	

Aims

The aims of this unit are to encourage you to think about:

1   how nineteenth-century states defined themselves both to each other and to their citizens;

2   where sovereignty lay in the states, and the debates about sovereignty;

3   how the citizens of the states were defined; and

4   the debates over the duties and rights of citizens.

It may be useful before you start this unit to refresh your memory of changing borders by referring to Video 1, pp.21–127.

The definitions of borders

In the early twentieth century Max Weber (1864–1920), the German sociologist, defined the state as a collection of institutions enjoying a monopoly of legitimate violence within a continuously bounded territory. The question is, how did the borders of a nineteenth-century state come to be recognized? With Great Britain the situation was relatively simple in as much as she was bounded by the sea. But there were, of course, the separate countries of England, Scotland and Wales on one of the British Isles, which had been united under the English monarchy following centuries of wars and treaties – the final treaty uniting England and Scotland was enacted in 1707. Ireland, a physically separate island, was also a part of Great Britain and subject to the British crown; again the links went back for centuries, but the final Act of Union was only passed in 1801.

On continental Europe the borders of one state had to be agreed with its neighbours, generally through some form of treaty. Even when there was broad agreement between statesmen, lines could still have to be drawn on the ground. Rivers made fairly obvious divides; mountains might seem a similar, logical division, but mountains can spread over a large area of territory. In 1816 the government in Restoration France set up two commissions to delineate the country's northern and eastern frontiers, both of which had changed considerably during the revolutionary and Napoleonic period. The northern commission finished its work in 1820, and the necessary agreements were then signed with the neighbouring powers; resolution of the eastern frontiers took several more years.

The Pyrenees were traditionally acknowledged as the frontier with Spain, and, while there had been fighting in this region, no commission was appointed here in the aftermath of the Napoleonic wars. Increasingly, however, governments on both sides of the mountains began to experience problems. The peasants in the Cerdagne border area, for example, were all Catalan. Contraband poured in both directions. The French government was also regularly concerned by the civil upheavals in Spain as they threatened to cross the unmarked frontier. Boundary commissioners were eventually appointed in the early 1850s, who promptly perceived another problem. As the Spanish commissioners explained in June 1852:

> In vain can we say to men: this or that is your nationality, this is your fatherland, that is your history, only because here or there stands a mountain which defines a water shed; in vain can we tell them, 'we will change your name, because there is a barrier which divides you' … these people will not believe us. (quoted in Sahlins, 1989, p.247)

Furthermore, while boundary commissioners might come up with one set of problems, generals urged frontiers which were defensible and made military sense with reference to the protection of the state. Thus, in March 1866, as decisions on the actual line of the Franco-Spanish border began to be settled, the French minister of war wrote to the foreign minister:

I am astonished and worried to see the definition of the frontier of France and Spain submit itself to the habits, customs, and claims of small Pyrenean communes; the dividing line twists and turns carefully so as not to bother these communities, instead of following a general rule dictated by great interests far superior to local quarrels. (quoted in Sahlins, 1989, p.250)

END NAP WARS
CONGRESS OF VIENNA

The final treaty was eventually signed in 1868, and while it did try to take the interests of communities and individuals into account, it nevertheless did end up leaving small areas of land on the 'wrong' side of the border as far as many local inhabitants were concerned.

The set text of this course (Anderson) begins with the end of the Napoleonic wars in 1815. The end of these wars saw the leading statesmen of the powers of Europe sitting down at the Congress of Vienna to agree the map of Europe and the territories of the particular states.

Exercise   Read Anderson, p.1, and then answer the following questions.

1   What were the aims of the statesmen at Vienna?

2   How did they set out to achieve them?

3   What part, if any, does nationality appear to have played in their decisions?

4   Can you think of any reasons why this was so?

For questions 3 and 4 you will probably find it helpful to turn again to the maps which you consulted in the introduction to the course (see Maps 1 and 3 in the Maps Booklet).

Specimen Answers and   You probably came up with the following:
Discussion

CONGRESS OF
VIENNA 1815

1   The statesmen sought to establish a balance of power, preventing any single state or ruler from establishing domination over the others.

2   They restored (and restrained) the old French monarchy, and sought to balance the respective size and strengths of the different states.

3   There is no mention of nationality in Anderson's discussion here, and given the way in which states gained control of territories which do not appear to belong to them in any logical, 'national' sense (most obviously Polish lands in Russia, but also the Rhineland as part of Prussia, and Genoa as part of what Anderson calls Savoy-Sardinia, but which is more generally referred to as Sardinia-Piedmont, ruled by the house of Savoy), nationality does not appear to have figured much in the statesmen's deliberations.

4   Making decisions on the basis of nationality would have created a problem for the Austrian Empire with its multitude of nationalities. But there is also the question as to where any such decisions based on nationality might have stopped. Rhinelanders, like Prussians, were Germans, and Genoese, like the other inhabitants of Sardinia-Piedmont, were Italians; but it was hardly conceivable that statesmen, keen to establish a balance of power after over twenty years of war, would want to generate further upheavals by creating new, large nation states.

It would be useful to make two points here.

First, there are several references in my answers, and in Anderson, to 'balance of power'. This was a term used by contemporaries, and it meant, broadly, ensuring that no power should be able to dominate Europe as France had done under Napoleon. What was never precisely resolved, however, was the key question: who was to judge when the balance was upset? In the event, the period following Napoleon was mercifully free of similar individuals with similar opportunities, and consequently the problem did not arise. The Crimean War, the next armed conflict to involve several great powers after the fall of Napoleon, can be seen as an attempt to maintain the balance of power, but there were also a variety of other issues involved. Russia, for example, could claim to be protecting European Christians from Muslim Turks by interfering to protect the Christian holy places in the Ottoman Empire. Britain was clearly worried about Russian moves towards her interests in the near east and, especially, India. France had financial interests in the Ottoman Empire. Austria backed Britain and France in the war, concerned that Russia should not be allowed to see the break up of the Ottoman Empire as something confined to Russia's backyard – Austria too had frontiers with the Turks.

Secondly, limiting national aspirations at Vienna in 1815, like limiting liberal ideology, was central to the way that several of the key statesmen in Restoration Europe understood their task. On occasions this led them to ignore the sanctity of borders.

Exercise   Turn now to your Documents Collection. Read Document I.1 and answer the following questions:

1   What do the signatories promise each other by this alliance?

2   How do the signatories believe that their subjects should behave?

3   What does Anderson have to say about this document on p.2?

Specimen Answers   1   They promise mutual assistance to any one of their number under threat.

2   They believe that their subjects should be quiescent and accept the status quo.

3   Anderson states that, in the event, the Holy Alliance was rather more a declaration of intent than a firm agreement.

⚡ Anderson notes that the British foreign secretary, Lord Castlereagh (1769–1822), was unmoved by the Holy Alliance – in fact he called it 'sublime mysticism and nonsense'. For Metternich (1773–1859) it was 'a loud sounding nothing' (quoted in Hinsley, 1963, p.196), but he did view the situation in Europe rather differently from Castlereagh.

Exercise   Read Document I.2 and answer the following questions:

1   What does Metternich consider here to be the problem facing Europe?

2   What is the cause of this problem?

3   Which social group is to blame?

4   Which country stands out as the exception in Metternich's understanding?

5   What is the solution?

Specimen Answers   1   Metternich considers the whole structure of Europe to be under threat.

2   The problem is that progress and knowledge have led to 'presumption' on the part of some men. What I think you might find particularly interesting to note here is how, in the paragraph beginning 'Religion, morality, legislation, economy ...', Metternich is expressing his concerns about things which, today, are accepted as the basis for a liberal democracy.

3   The middle classes are the group primarily responsible for pressing these ideas.

4   England, where a long tradition of a representative institution and where, in consequence, the 'presumption' of this social group leads to demands for 'reform' rather than something more extreme.

5   The only solution for the powers of Europe is strong, vigorous government to maintain stability; he says also that such government should be beneficent as well as strict.

Now I have just asked you to draw some straightforward points out of this document; I will ask you similar questions in this unit and others. These points were transparent and unproblematic, but historians cannot always use documents in such a straightforward way. I have asked you what Metternich wrote; the next question, of course, is was he right? and how did his fears and prejudices inform his interpretation. These are points that you should tease out for yourself as we move on through the unit and look at those who Metternich considered 'presumptuous'. But remember too that Metternich was not alone in his assumptions about the dangers facing Europe.

Exercise   Read Document I.3 and answer the following question:

1   To what are the signatories agreeing here?

Specimen Answer   1   To intervene in those states where there are changes of government as a result of revolutions.

TROPPAU
PROTOCOL

TREATY OF
MÜNCHENGRÄTZ
(AUSTRIA/RUSSIA)

BORDER
ADJUSTMENTS.

OTTOMAN
EMPIRE.

TREATY OF
BERLIN

The Troppau Protocol was agreed against the background of revolution in the Kingdom of Naples and in Spain. It would be wrong to believe that the kind of intervention promised in the document became a common-place in the first half of the nineteenth century, but there were several instances. Austrian troops were deployed early in 1821 to suppress the revolution in Naples; a few months later they crushed a similar revolt in Piedmont. Although the French and British governments shared concerns about the protocol, the French chose, in April 1823, to send 95,000 troops into Spain to 'restore order'. The potential for trouble in their respective Polish territories led Austria and Russia to agreeing, in September 1833, the treaty of Münchengrätz which promised mutual aid in case of uprising. It was in the spirit of the Münchengrätz treaty that Tsar Nicholas I (1796–1855) sent military assistance to help Austria suppress the Hungarian Revolution of 1848–9.

The second half of the century witnessed a few border adjustments in western and central Europe as the result of wars and treaties. The internal frontiers on the Italian peninsula were dissolved as the wars of independence transformed Italy into a nation state. Wars within, and on the frontiers of the German lands, altered both their internal and external shape: Austria was excluded from 'Germany' and Prussia became the sole, dominant power; and, following the French defeat in 1871, Alsace and Lorraine were added to Germany. But the key border changes were to be found in the Balkans, and it was here that concerns about the 'balance of power' led to concerted action by the great powers against one of their number, and the significant redrawing of frontiers.

The Ottoman Empire's hold on the Balkans was progressively weakened throughout the nineteenth century. As Figure 1 shows, Serbia had gained limited autonomy in 1812, and this was extended in 1830, the year in which Greece won her independence. Moldavia and Wallachia gained autonomy in 1833. The greatest changes, however, came in the 1870s. In 1876 there was an uprising against Turkish rule in Bulgaria. Serbia and Montenegro joined in. The Ottoman Empire, having to cope also with a palace revolt in Constantinople, responded with ferocity; its troops massacred Bulgarian peasants by the thousand. Russia prepared to march to the aid of her fellow Slavs. Russia had only recently (1873) entered into an agreement with Austria-Hungary and Germany – the *Dreikaiserbund* (the league of the three emperors) to maintain the status quo in Europe. Bismarck saw this as a way of keeping France isolated after her defeat in the Franco-Prussian War, but for Austria-Hungary and Russia it was primarily a way of reducing the mutual suspicion between the two, particularly in the Balkans where both sides had frontiers and, consequently, an interest in what happened to the Ottoman Empire. Austria-Hungary agreed to Russian intervention on the side of the Bulgarians on the condition that the Russians did not turn the war into a Pan-Slav crusade. The court at Vienna also agreed to frustrate any efforts by Britain to resolve the issue by invoking an earlier treaty. Flushed with victory over the Turks, however, the Russians reneged on the understanding. They imposed the Treaty of San Stefano (3 March 1878) on the Ottoman Empire creating a 'Big Bulgaria' between the Aegean and the Black Seas. The other powers of Europe, suspicious that this new state would be a Russian puppet, united at the Congress of Berlin to bring about the Treaty of Berlin (13 July 1878). The treaty put the north-western province of the Ottoman

Dates refer to the year in which independence was gained from Turkey.

Territory lost by Turkey as a result of the Balkan War of 1913.

RUSSIA

AUSTRIA–HUNGARY

Bessarabia

Jassy

Moldavia Autonomous 1822

1878

RUMANIA

BOSNIA
Austrian Territory
Sarajevo

Belgrade

1878

Bucharest

Wallachia
Autonomous 1822

Dobrudja 1878

1913 from Bulgaria

Black Sea

SERBIA

1913 from Serbia
1830

Aleksinatz
1876

Nish

Plevna
1877

1878

Sofia

Burgas

MONTE–NEGRO
independent
since 1389

ALBANIA

Kumanova
1912

1885

Adrianople

Kirk Kilisse 1912
Lule Burgas 1912

BULGARIA

Durazzo

MACEDONIA
1913

1913

Ochrid

Salonika

1913

Constantinople

Adriatic Sea

CORFU
English 1814–63;
Greek 1863

1881–1897

Aegean
Sea

Smyrna

ITALY

GREECE

Missolonghi 1826

Athens

1830

TURKEY

Mediterranean Sea

Navarino
1827

DODECANESE
(Italian 1912)

CRETE
(Greek 1913)

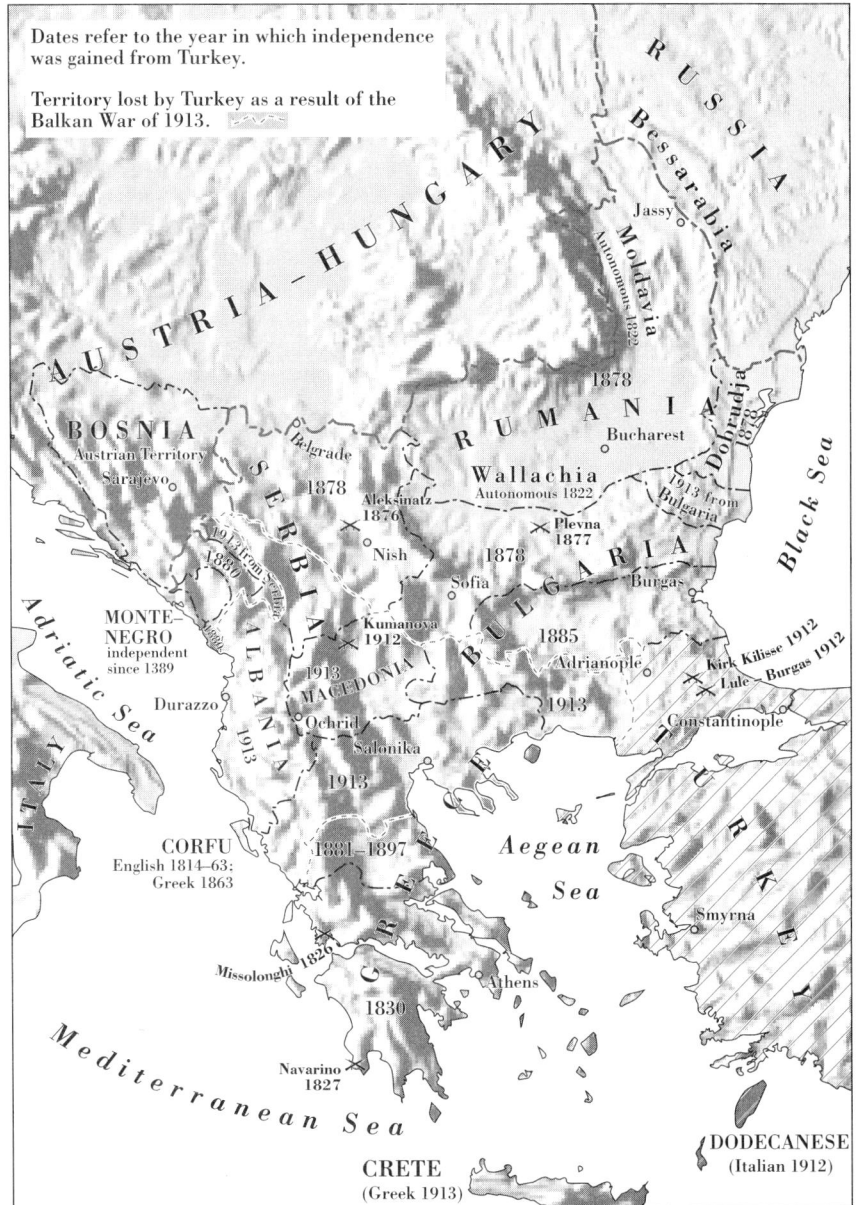

Figure 1
The Balkans during the
nineteenth century.
*(Reproduced from M.
Gilbert*, Recent History
Atlas, 1860 to 1960,
*Weidenfeld and Nicolson,
p. 13.)*

Empire, Bosnia-Herzegovina, under Austro-Hungarian occupation. It recognized Bulgaria, Romania and Serbia as independent states, but Bulgaria was considerably reduced in size with most of the territory between Bulgaria and Greece being returned to the Ottoman Empire, apart from an area which was attached to Serbia. This left a legacy of anger and frustration among the Bulgarians; in 1885 they united the autonomous territory of East Rumelia with their state, and defeated a Serbian army sent to maintain the Balkan balance of power. In 1912, and again in 1913, rivalries between these new states and between them and their former Ottoman ruler flared again into war.

NEW BALKAN
STATES - ETHNIC
MIX

A key problem in the new Balkan states was that, while provinces may have had some long-standing recognition under the Ottoman Empire, there was a tremendous ethnic mix within them. The frontiers drawn by the statesmen of the great powers took little note of this problem, indeed it is unlikely that they would have recognized the difference between Bulgarians and Macedonians, both Slav peoples, or between them and Romanians, who were not. The new Balkan states claimed to be nation states, and their national leaders tended to speak only for the dominant national group within the territory; but they also cast covetous eyes on the territories of their neighbours inhabited by their ethnic kin.

Constitutions

Drawing up and agreeing frontiers was one thing, but deciding how states were to be run internally was another. It might involve external participation, especially when, as during the Restoration period, proposed changes upset conservative and interventionist-minded great powers. Generally speaking, however, the structure of internal administration and government was an internal matter. Much continued to depend upon historical development and the way in which institutions had evolved within the different states. But the eighteenth century had witnessed considerable intellectual debate about how men should be governed, as well as their rights and duties within the state. The American and French Revolutions provided examples of legislative institutions formulating constitutions, and of governments seeking to rule through them. The French Revolution, in the person of Napoleon, was eventually defeated, and the United States remained distant, several weeks sailing from Europe, but the idea of written constitutions stipulating governmental forms and the rights and duties of citizens remained potent in Restoration Europe – witness Metternich's concerns in Document I.2. When the Bourbon monarchy was restored to France in 1814, after more than twenty years, Louis XVIII (1755–1824) thought it expedient to issue the Constitutional Charter for his subjects.

IDEA OF WRITTEN
CONSTITUTION
LIKE IN US,
POTENT IN
RESTORATION
EUROPE.

Exercise

Turn to your Documents Collection, read the extracts from the Constitutional Charter (I.4) and answer the following questions:

1   What kind of state is being defined here?

2   On what does this state base its legitimacy?

3   From where do the people of the state get their rights?

4   What limits are there on the authority of the monarch?

Specimen Answers

1   A monarchy, in which sovereignty is vested in the king.

2   Legitimacy here, though never discussed as such, is largely based on historical precedent with references to Louis XVIII being 'brought back' to his kingdom, and references to the actions of his predecessors in whose tradition he is following. The very beginning of the preamble suggests also, perhaps, a degree of divine authority which has restored the king to his throne.

FRANCE
CONSTITUTIONAL
CHARTER.
4 JUNE 1814

3   People's rights are granted by courtesy of the monarch.

4   There are no limits specified to the king's powers, indeed the preamble states that his first duty was to maintain 'the rights and prerogatives of the crown', though this, it is stressed, is for the benefit of his people.

Exercise

CONSTITUTIONAL
CHARTER 1830 -
MODIFYING 1814 .

Now read Document I.5 and answer the following questions:

1   What body is responsible for this revision?

2   How does this document make the state a different kind of monarchy?

3   What limitations are now put on the monarch?

4   How would you characterize this new monarchy?

Specimen Answers

1   The chamber of deputies has made the revision.

2   The deputies specifically suppress the idea of the monarch granting rights to the people and require the king, and his successors, to agree to the charter before being invited to accept the crown.

3   Article 13 specifically states that the monarch cannot suspend or dispense with any laws.

4   I suppose that the monarchy is best described as 'limited' or 'constitutional', though its predecessor was also constitutional especially in relation to those further east in Europe. A 'liberal monarchy' might be a more accurate description; the popular historical description of the reign of Louis Philippe is 'the bourgeois monarchy'.

REV - TO
REMOVE CHARLES X
FROM FRENCH
THRONE .

This revision followed the French Revolution of 1830. Louis XVIII's brother, Charles X (1757–1836), had succeeded to the throne in 1824. Much more conservative, and less inclined to compromise than his brother, Charles brought about the revolution through his own actions. The people who participated in the street fighting in Paris in July 1830 were not intent on creating Louis Philippe, Duke of Orléans (1773–1850), as their new king. The principal aim was the removal of Charles X; some were republicans, others were probably Bonapartists (Napoleon's son, the Duke of Reichstadt (1811–32), sometimes known as Napoleon II, was still alive and had been brought up as an Austrian prince). There were others, particularly among the respectable bourgeoisie who had not taken to the streets, but who had served in the assembly, or who ran the country's administration and its business and financial concerns, who were pleased to see Charles X removed, but who dreaded a repetition of the Jacobin terror of the earlier revolution. It was these men, at the centre of power in Paris, who eagerly brought Louis Philippe forward, not as 'king of France,' but as 'king of the French.' The change in title suggested less the possessor of a territory whose inhabitants were his subjects, and rather more the first citizen among others.

Exercise   Now read Document I.6 and answer the following questions:

CONSTITUTION

NOV 1848

1   What form of state is established by this document?

2   How does the content here extend the idea of sovereignty from the charter of 1830?

3   Can you see any articles indicating a new kind of relationship between the state and the citizen?

Specimen Answers and Discussion

1   A <u>republic.</u>

2   Sovereignty is now rooted in the French people with all men having the vote. The people delegate executive and legislative power; justice is rendered in the people's name; the head of state is now specifically answerable before the law.

3   Articles VI, VII and VIII stipulate reciprocal duties between the citizen and the state; duties which are not apparent in the preceding documents.

SEEM PROG

– BUT BE CAUTIOUS

Louis Philippe's government became increasingly conservative and unpopular and, in 1848, the bourgeois monarchy, like its predecessor, was overthrown by street fighting in Paris. These documents – the Constitutional Charter, the 1830 revision, and the Constitution of 1848 – are increasingly progressive, but you must beware of perceiving the history of nineteenth-century France, or anywhere else for that matter, as advancing simply and inexorably on a progressive track.

2ND REP 1848

↓

2ND EMP OF NAP III

↓

3RD REP

The Second Republic established in 1848 was followed, within five years, by the Second Empire of Napoleon III (1808–73). Napoleon maintained a populist facade to his regime, most notably by the use of the plebiscite, but in reality France was subjected once again to authoritarian rule. The Second Empire fell as a result of military defeat in the Franco-Prussian War, and out of the shambles of that defeat and the savage violence of the Paris Commune, a new republic emerged. There was no specific constitution for the Third Republic, but a series of constitutional laws in 1875 established the executive (a president) and the legislature (a senate and a chamber of deputies). These laws made no mention of the sovereignty of the people, but they did enable the president to be impeached before the legislature.

BRITAIN

HISTORY BOOK –

"CONSTITUTIONAL

HISTORY"

Exercise   I want now to cross the Channel to Britain. Read Document I.7, and then answer the following:

1   What sort of document is this?

2   Given that the preceding documents were constitutions proper, why do you suppose I have used this particular kind of document to discuss the British constitution?

3   What limits are imposed on the monarch by law?

4   What is it that qualifies a man to vote in Britain, and how does this contrast with the various constitutional situations in France?

5   What significant change does Maitland detect occurring in parliament over the preceding fifty years?

Specimen Answers   1   It is a history book, based on a course of lectures designed for lawyers ('we are lawyers dealing with law').

2   There is no written British constitution. Maitland illustrates the point with, for example, a reference to the cabinet, which is not established by law, but has evolved by custom and convention.

3   Maitland suggests that there have been remarkably few limitations imposed on the monarch by law since the reign of Henry VII (1457–1509). The situation has changed, he insists, though pinpointing exactly how can be a matter of dispute.

4   *Legally*, according to Maitland's interpretation, a man in Britain was qualified to vote only by appearing on the electoral register (oh, the wonderful complexities of legal-speak!), and this register has a variety of other uses. However, to have his name on the register, the man had to have some relationship with real property. In the first two French constitutions which you looked at, the vote was tied to a man's tax assessment; but in the Republic of 1848, it became a man's right as a citizen.

5   Maitland believes that over the preceding fifty years parliament has begun to legislate much more than to govern. It has established general rules for others, endowed with new statutory powers, to follow.

There is nothing about rights in any of the passages extracted from Maitland, indeed there is little about rights in his description of the constitution. Sovereignty lay, not with the people, but with parliament. This was primarily because of the way that the British constitution had evolved, in its unwritten form, avoiding the upheavals of continental Europe. During the French Revolution Edmund Burke (1729–97), perhaps the most significant conservative publicist of all time, had urged the excellence of the British constitution precisely for its organic quality. It was folly, he maintained, to attempt to draft constitutions from scratch. The victory over Napoleon (and thus indirectly over the ideas of the French Revolution) strengthened satisfaction with the constitution; and so too did Britain's general avoidance of the revolutions which wracked continental Europe in 1830 and 1848.

There were serious riots preceding the Great Reform Act of 1832 and, on a much lesser scale, there were disorders before the reform act of 1867. There could also be turbulent behaviour during parliamentary elections, though this declined as the century wore on. In the first half of the century radicals and Chartists did not demand a new constitution, but the removal of what they considered to be abuses and injustices which had been introduced into it by corrupt ministers.

FRANCHISE
REFORM.

During the debates on reform in the mid-1860s Liberals, like Gladstone (1809–98), envisaged the franchise being extended to incorporate men from the working class as they became better educated and informed; and it was a minority Conservative government which, guided by Disraeli (1804–81), passed the second reform act in 1867. Victorians believed in gradual but steady progress; until quite recently the historians who studied nineteenth-century constitutional developments in Britain tended to take them at their word and to chart a steady pattern of advance from 1832 through to the reform act of 1918 which finally enfranchised all adult males and also women over thirty. You might, of course, query whether progress over eighty-six years indicates advance at anything other than a snail's pace.

IRELAND
UNHAPPY

But even accepting the traditional interpretation, there was one significant problem to Britain's constitutional progress. In Ireland many remained unhappy with the 1801 union and sought some restoration of autonomy. The movement for Home Rule gathered strength in the later decades of the nineteenth century and split the Liberal Party. There was also a minority of Irishmen who called for independence and backed their demands with sporadic violence; on two occasions, in 1867 and 1883–4, this violence spilled over into a bombing campaign in England.

LIBERAL
STATE.

Although Britain was perceived to some extent as a liberal state, this was not because it had a constitution based on notions of the natural rights of man and the sovereignty of the people. There were legal safeguards for the subjects of the British monarch – for example, there was the Habeas Corpus Act which could be used to prevent arrest without charge, there was the general right to a trial before a jury of a man's peers, there was a considerable degree of religious liberty (particularly following the repeal of the Test Acts in 1828 and Catholic emancipation the following year) and of press freedom. There also appears to have been an ethos among the British ruling élite that they were, somehow, different and more liberal than their continental neighbours, which ensured that they acted with the law and the constitutions; in short, they believed their own rhetoric.

Exercise Read Anderson, pp.62–4, and answer the following questions:

1   Can you see any theoretical similarity between the British and Russian cases?

2   What was the difference in practice between the two?

Specimen Answers 1   In neither state was there any legal check on the power of the monarch.

2   In practice in Britain there were significant checks established by custom and precedent (remember Maitland) and by the rise of a strong, self-confident parliament (Anderson, p.62); in Russia there were no such checks.

PARLIAMENT —

VICTORIA HAD
TO REPLACE
MELBOURNE WITH
PEEL.

A good example of the checks on the British monarchy created by precedent and a self-confident parliament was the situation with regards to appointing a prime minister. Queen Victoria (1819–1901) had come to the throne in 1837 when Lord Melbourne (1779–1848) was prime minister. He had carefully, and successfully, instructed her in her role as queen. She, in turn, was extremely reluctant to let him go even as his parliamentary majority was reduced and when, in June 1841, his government lost a vote of confidence after its budget had been rejected. She urged him to go to the country rather than resign. Melbourne lost the ensuing election and Victoria was compelled to invite Sir Robert Peel (1788–1850), leader of the Tories whom she intensely disliked, to form a government. While, generally, her predecessors had chosen their prime ministers with little reference to the result of elections, in this situation, with the Whig government floundering and a deficit mounting, she had no choice. *The Times* noted the significance: 'the world has never known an instance of a party being installed in power ... solely because the nation pledges confidence in their capacity and disinterestedness' (quoted in Gash, 1972, p.266). Admittedly there was no other example of a government being changed as the result of a general election between the reform acts of 1832 and 1867; and no government with a working majority was overthrown in an election until 1874 when Disraeli replaced Gladstone; but the significant precedent had been set.

Exercise

CARBONARI

KAKHOVSKY JUSTIFICATION
FOR THE DECEMBRIST
INSURRECTION 1826.

Now read Documents I.8 and I.9 and answer the following:

1 In what ways might these documents be said to fit in with the anxiety expressed by Metternich in his Confession of Faith (Document I.2)?

2 Can you see any broadly similar aspirations between the aims of the Society of Guelf Knights and Kakhovsky?

3 How does Kakhovsky consider the people to have been betrayed?

4 Where, particularly, does Kakhovsky find his inspiration?

Specimen Answers

BOTH
WANT LIBERALIZATION
OF REGIMES.

FRENCH REV —
INSPIRATION.

1 They are both referring to secret societies (Metternich's 'gangrene of society'), one outlining the aims and methods of a society of *Carbonari* in Italy, the other the proud confession of a Russian revolutionary. Kakhovsky is conscious in his confession of belonging to a wider movement for liberty across the whole of Europe.

2 They are both seeking a liberalization of the regimes in which they live. Kakhovsky makes continual references to 'liberty' and pronounces the 'sacred truth – that [people] do not exist for governments, but that governments must be organized for them'. The *Carbonari* seek a basic liberal constitution.

3 He maintains that they were given promises by their monarch during the wars against Napoleon, but then the promises were ignored.

4 The French Revolution.

SECRET SOCIETIES-
NOT MUCH THREAT.

Anderson (pp.71–2) discusses the *Carbonari*, and their French equivalents the *Charbonnerie*. The movement appears to have spread across the length and breadth of Europe, but as Anderson stresses, secret societies were never much of a threat. As the historian of their 'mythology' noted:

> Evidence about the growth and expansion of these societies poured in to the governments of [Restoration] Europe; nowhere were they eradicated. This caused much alarm, led to more publicity, and then to more alarm. No one seemed to notice that the secret societies never succeeded in doing anything which would justify the attention given to them. They justified neither the hopes nor the fears they aroused. (Roberts, 1974, pp.320–1)

(Remember that earlier I asked you to think about Metternich's assumptions, and whether he was right in his Confession of Faith.)

RUSSIANS AFTER
WAR WANTED
CHANGE - 1818
"UNION OF WELFARE"

The society which Kakhovsky describes, however, was not a group of *Carbonari*. Following the defeat of Napoleon many young Russian army officers returned from the wars with ideas about improving their country; in particular they wanted to abolish serfdom and redistribute the land; some sought a constitutional monarchy, others contemplated a republic. They organized in small, secret groups of which the most significant was the Union of Salvation. In 1818 this group changed its name to the Union of Welfare and divided in two, with a southern and northern branch. The former branch was the more radical. But even one of the leaders of the more moderate northern branch, Nikita M. Muraviev, could draft a constitution beginning:

THEIR
CONSTITUTION

1   The Russian people are free and independent, and consequently are not, and cannot be, the property of any individual or family.

2   The source of *supreme power* is the people, who have exclusive right to make *fundamental laws* for themselves.

He went on to describe 'citizenship' as:

> ... the right to participate, in accordance with the rules set forth in this Constitution, in the government – either indirectly, that is through the election of officials or electors, or directly, that is through being elected to any public office of the legislative, executive or judicial branches. (quoted in Dmytryshyn, 1974, p.184)

DECEMBERISTS
REVOLTED —
EXILED .

When Tsar Alexander (1777–1825) died in December 1825, there was confusion over the succession. The leaders of the secret societies launched an ill-considered, unplanned revolt. The Decembrists, as the revolutionaries became known, expected mass support; but it never came. The revolt was suppressed within twenty-four hours. Five leaders, including Kakhovsky, were executed; the others were exiled.

Exercise   Read Anderson from the bottom of p.72 to p.80, and answer the following.

1   What does Anderson consider to have been more successful than the secret societies in challenging the conservative monarchies?

2   Where did this pressure come from?

Specimen Answers 1   A growing pressure for effective parliamentary government.

2   Anderson mentions this pressure coming from several directions: the ideas of the French revolution (and to this extent we might conclude that the secret societies were only the most extreme manifestation of this pressure); a growing radicalism within the universities of continental Europe; a growing public opinion on political issues, fostered by developments in communications.

There is, perhaps, an implication in Anderson that the monarchies of Europe and the old order were standing shoulder to shoulder against this pressure. This was not always the case. There are instances of monarchs and their principal ministers seeking to modernize their states and borrowing some of the trappings of constitutionalism themselves to undermine the remaining vestiges of feudalism. This kind of thing is noticeable, for example, in parts of what has been dubbed 'the third Germany' – those medium-sized states which developed under Napoleonic hegemony.

Reforms here, began during the Napoleonic period, were continued under the restoration. The monarchs and their ministers whittled away at the privileges of the *Standesherren* (the knights of the old Holy Roman Empire) and set out to create a citizenry subject to clear and uniform obligations to government. In 1806 Baron Marschall von Bieberstein, the chief minister of Nassau, noted the need to ensure that the knights could not be allowed to exist as 'a state within a state'. They had to become only 'rich property owners within the state, equipped with a few privileges ... but without infringing upon the unity of the state'. As for abolishing the feudal dues exacted from the peasantry and establishing a more rational fiscal system, this would not only improve the economy, but 'the inhabitants who are so hard pressed by intolerable manorial obligations will love and cherish the government which makes them into free human beings' (quoted in Anderson, 1991, pp.235 and 237). This, of course, was a way of strengthening the central power of the state and was something which absolutist monarchs had been doing since the seventeenth century at least.

However, the abolition of fiscal and legal privileges, and the creation of a rough form of equality before the law, were part of the liberal demands; and these often went together with the granting of constitutions on the lines of that granted by Louis XVIII to France in 1814. Constitutions in the third Germany were granted in Saxe-Weimar in 1814, and renewed in 1816, in Baden and Bavaria in 1818, in Württemberg in 1819, in Hesse-Darmstadt in 1820. A cluster of revolutions across Europe in 1830 were defeated, but, according to their historian, made 'pure absolutism harder to sustain' (Church, 1983, p.176) and were followed by a clutch of new constitutions in, again sticking to Germany, Brunswick, Hesse-Kassel, Hanover and Saxony.

I want to move on now to look at constitutions during the revolutions of 1848.

Exercise   Read Anderson pp.92–5, and then Documents I.10 and I.11. In what ways do these two documents reflect a continuance of the kind of debates which we witnessed in France?

Discussion   They reveal a conflict over where the seat of sovereignty was situated. Charles Albert is *granting* the constitution to his people, but maintaining his position as the executive with considerable control over the running of the state. Mazzini's Roman Republic, in contrast, is rooted in the belief of the sovereignty of the people.

As you will see from the headnote to Document I.10, the constitution presented to the people of Piedmont was rather more the product of a fear of revolution than any altruism on Charles Albert's part. His absolutist ministers resigned on its introduction, to be replaced by a government headed by a moderate Italian nationalist, Count Cesare Balbo; but the king was determined to hold on to as much power as possible. Eventually his constitution was to become the basis for that of the united Italy which was finally established under his successor, Victor Emanuel II (1820–78).

The Roman Republic lasted only a few months, but it was noted for its tolerance and enlightenment – something of a challenge, perhaps to Anderson's assertion (p.93) that there were always irreconcilable presuppositions between liberalism (admittedly in this instance of a pretty radical variety) and nationalism. In spite of a brilliant defence directed by the other great nineteenth-century radical Italian nationalist who, like Mazzini, stands out for his honesty and integrity – Giuseppe Garibaldi (1807–82) – the city fell to a siege conducted by regular French troops intent on restoring the pope.

Anderson notes (p.92) that while there was no national body created in Italy in 1848, such an institution was established in Germany in the shape of the Frankfurt Parliament.

Exercise   Read Document I.12 and answer the following questions:

1   What kind of state is this seeking to create?

2   Where does sovereignty lie?

3   What is there that is politically liberal about this document?

4   Where might nationalism be said to be acquiring a dominance over liberalism in the document?

Specimen Answers   1   A federal state incorporating the independent states of Germany.

2   In the Reich Authority. It is not precisely stated in the constitution exactly what this authority is, or where it comes from. It is not sovereignty of the people. There is to be a parliament, but it is not explained how far the parliament is to have any control or supervision of the Reich ministers, though it can impeach them. Article XII requires representative assemblies in the different states of the Reich, to which ministers are responsible, but the extent of this responsibility is not defined.

3   The 'basic rights' guaranteed to the German people are, generally speaking, the kinds of things which liberals sought. The constitution promises, for example, equality before the law, the abolition of serfdom, and freedom of assembly, conscience and the press.

4   Section 1 of the constitution deals in general terms with the Reich, with German and non-German states, and with German citizenship. Thus, rather than the rights of man, the initial emphasis of the constitution was on the rights of German citizens to be ruled only by German citizens if they are resident in German lands.

The Liberals of the Frankfurt Parliament have been much criticized by historians for failure. But they had set themselves an impossible task. There were two major powers in Germany – Prussia and Austria; and while both were caught off-balance by the revolutions of 1848, neither became sympathetic towards liberalism. Moreover had one of the two powers accepted the position of Head of the Reich, was it really conceivable that the other would meekly accept its resulting inferiority? As Anderson (p.92) explains, the parliament offered the crown to Frederick William IV of Prussia (1795–1861) in April 1849. The king's generals and ministers were opposed, but Frederick William himself was tempted. In the end, however, he declined to accept the offer unless it came from his fellow German princes; accepting the crown from a group of elected deputies was far too democratic in his eyes. When Germany was finally united into a federated empire in 1871, with the king of Prussia as emperor, a new constitution was prepared. It was not greatly dissimilar from the constitution that was prepared by the Frankfurt Assembly, but there was no requirement to harmonize the constitutions of the Federal states and there was no section on the rights of citizens. Most important, however, the circumstances of unification were very different. Unification followed a victorious war against France under Prussian leadership and was the product of an agreement by consenting princes, rather than people; furthermore the dominant power, Prussia, was ruled under a constitution which greatly limited the power of elected representatives.

A relatively liberal constitution had been drafted for Prussia during the revolution of 1848. But in December 1848 Frederick William had dissolved the Prussian parliament and proclaimed a new constitution which, together, with new legislation introduced in the following months, was designed to tighten the grip of the old order. The basic civil rights and duties, such as equality before the law, freedom of conscience, association and assembly were left unaltered. The parliament of two chambers was also kept with its upper house nominated by the king, and its elected lower house. Elections to the lower house were indirect and based on a three-class franchise which favoured the wealthy. Thus, while all taxpaying men who had reached the age of 24 and who were not in receipt of charity were enfranchised, the influence of those in the third class of lowest earners was greatly restricted. It was probably as a consequence of this that increasing numbers did not bother to vote. Ministers were appointed and dismissed by the king; there was no cabinet government with a principal minister. The position of chancellor was developed by Bismarck with the beginnings of federalism under the North German Confederation in 1867. Furthermore, in addition to his ministers, the king had personal advisers for various sections of the state who were kept far away from the parliament; most notable here was his military cabinet.

The early 1860s witnessed a constitutional struggle in Prussia which considerably weakened any potential for parliamentary opposition to the king and his ministers. Constitutionally the parliament had some influence over the budget; though taxes were established as permanent, the parliament voted on whether to authorize the expenditure proposed by the government. The size of the Prussian army had not changed since the reorganization of 1817. In 1861 General Albrecht von Roon, the war minister, sought to increase the army by requiring every man to serve a three-year period of conscription, and by incorporating the reserve into it. A majority in the lower chamber was agreeable – universal military service was regarded as a liberal institution – but it wanted the period of service kept to two years. When von Roon, supported by the king, refused, the chamber authorized the government's military expenditure for one year only expecting that the reforms would be postponed. In the following year, 1862, as von Roon pressed ahead with his reforms, the chamber went further and refused to sanction any expenditure. It was at this point that Bismarck (1815–98) was summoned to act as principal minister. On taking office Bismarck announced, in an oft-quoted passage, that the great questions of the day would not be resolved 'by speeches and the resolutions of majorities ... but by blood and iron'. He further formulated the theory of a 'hole' in the constitution.

The constitution, he noted, required the agreement of the king and parliament for any legislation, but it did not explain what was to happen when there was no such agreement. It was consequently necessary for the king to continue to rule, thus filling the 'hole', until a solution could be found. For the next four years Bismarck ruled Prussia in the name of the king but without parliament's agreement for any financial expenditure. The Liberals and the Progressives, who made up the intransigent majority in the lower house, sat tight hoping that Bismarck's policies, especially his foreign policy would fail, thus forcing his removal and a victory for parliament. In the event Bismarck's policies met with success after success. In 1866, following the victory over Austria, the Progressives lost seats in the elections; many Liberals switched to Bismarck's side and agreed to an act of indemnity for the preceding four years.

Exercise Read Anderson pp.100–5 and 107–17, and answer the following:

1 What difference does he note between the authoritarian governments of the period before 1848 and those of the second half of the century?

2 Which groups, according to Anderson, stand out most for their failures?

3 Where were the major exceptions to the general changes in authoritarian government?

Specimen Answers 1 Authoritarian governments after 1848 were much more flexible, they professed an interest in their peoples, and sought out at least an element of public popularity. As a result of this people as a whole across most of Europe believed that they were living in a period of increasing political liberty.

2   The parliamentary leadership and political parties in Italy and Germany.

3   The Austro-Hungarian and the Russian Empires.

It was all very well to have a constitution, even a liberal one, but the economic, political and social structure of a country, as well as specific events, could influence how constitutions worked, and developed, in practice. Perhaps, in this respect, Anderson is a little unfair on the political leaders and political parties of Italy. The constitution of united Italy was the *Statuto* of Charles Albert (Document I.10). This had left considerable authority in the king's hands, and this authority was strengthened by the short duration of governments. Ministers were appointed by the king, not by parliament, or as a result of parliamentary elections. The fall of a ministry led to the king consulting with leading politicians to see who might be called upon to form the next administration. Such consultations could also be influenced by court intrigues.

The Italian wars of unification had left losers, as well as winners. Cities like Naples were unhappy about losing their rank as a capital. There were southern nobles who had supported the Bourbon monarchy of Naples, some of whom moved to Rome and continued their opposition to the house of Savoy. They had a powerful ally in Pope Pius IX (1792–1878) who, throughout the 1860s looked askance at proposals to make Rome the capital of the kingdom. In the summer of 1870 he had succeeded in getting the constitution *Pastor aeternus* agreed within the Church which proclaimed papal infallibility. A few weeks later Italian troops entered the city; Pius became, in his own phrase, the 'prisoner of the Vatican', and denounced the Italian state as a 'usurper'. He, and his immediate successors, instructed good Italian Catholics not to vote in the usurper's elections, thus preventing the development of a national catholic party which might have acted as a counter-balance to the parliamentary Liberals.

There were also problems within the Italian parliament emanating from traditions and political practice. The deputies were closely tied to their constituents and were expected to work, primarily, in the local interest. This situation was most acute in the South where clientage was a way of life. (Remember the comments of Paul Ginsborg on Video 1, pp.951–1000.) Writing of Sicily in 1876 a Tuscan noble, Leopoldo Franchetti, explained that there 'all relationships are founded on the concept of individual interests and on obligations between individuals, to the exclusion of any social or public interest whatsoever' (quoted in Clark, 1984, p.60). Deputies who failed to bring home the bacon for their constituents risked not being re-elected; ministers who failed to comply with a deputy's request risked losing that deputy's vote in parliament. Thus while there were broad divisions between 'left' and 'right' – and remember that the 'right' was limited as a result of papal disapproval – the task of prime ministers was first and foremost to construct a majority with favours, and then hang on to it with more of the same. Some men, notably Agostino Depretis (1813–87) and later Giovanni Giolitti (1842–1928), became particularly competent at making the system work. But even had leading politicians had a burning desire to reform the system, it would have been extremely difficult, and perhaps impossible, to have started to resolve the problems and to have stayed in power long enough to see the reforms through.

The conflict between religion and the state's constitution was not something confined to Italy. In Spain conservatives linked the religious unity of the country to its greatness. No matter that she appeared to be slipping behind economically, it was Spain's glory to stand aside from the evil ideas that were dissolving other states and to maintain Catholicism as the state's religion; moreover freedom of conscience could only serve to undermine the rights and privileges of truth. The constitution of 1876, which tolerated other faiths, was condemned by both Spanish churchmen and the pope. Nevertheless it was under this constitution, which lasted for almost half a century, that the conservative politician, Antonio Cánovas (1828–97), sought to reshape Spanish politics on what he understood to be the British model; he required the king to read texts on British parliamentary procedure and engineered elections so that two parties alternated in government. (Again, think back to Video 1, pp.909–30, and Paul Preston's story about the town boss (*cacique*) in Grenada who accepted God's will that he had lost the election as a Liberal, but was nevertheless pleased to have won as a Conservative.)

In France too there was conflict between the Catholic Church and liberal and radical elements. A Concordat between the pope and Napoleon had been agreed in 1801; this had recognized Catholicism as the religion of most Frenchmen, had put the Church under a degree of state control and had resulted in members of the clergy looking more and more to Rome to defend their cause. Republicans tended to see the Church as a force for conservatism and believed that it had played no small part in delivering large numbers of votes to Bonapartist and royalist candidates in the elections held under universal manhood suffrage in 1848, 1849, 1851, 1852, 1870 and 1871. They also feared that the power of the Catholic Church was increasing given its freedom to run schools, and they looked warily on the reactionary 'prisoner of the Vatican' to whom Catholics owed their loyalty. As republicans became more and more dominant in the Third Republic so they began whittling away at the powers of the Church; there were new educational laws, the Sisters of Mercy were barred from working in hospitals, army chaplains were abolished, divorce was established. The culmination of these moves came in December 1905 with legislation guaranteeing freedom of worship, but by which the state itself refused to recognize or subsidize any form of worship and reorganized the way in which church finances were organized – a move which led, ultimately, to the sequestration of church property.

You may have noted that the countries discussed in the preceding paragraphs – France, Italy, Spain – were all predominantly Catholic. The nineteenth-century state became increasingly egotistical, refusing to tolerate any supra-national body making similar claims to its own. Religious toleration, on the surface a liberal measure, could be part and parcel of this. For the state religion became a matter of individual conscience. Earlier I quoted Baron von Bliebenstein's determination that the *Standesherren* should not be allowed to be a state within a state; the Catholic Church found itself in the same situation.

The French experience during the Third Republic also provides a good example of how political events could lead to a significant shift of power within the structure established by a written constitution. The early period of the Republic is known as 'the republic of the dukes'. The elections following the defeat in the Franco-Prussian war and then the uprising of the Paris Commune, produced a majority of monarchists in the assembly. These were divided between supporters of the Legitimist and Orleanist claimants, and even when a compromise seemed probable on 'Henri V' (the Count of Chambord; 1820–83), the Legitimist heir, the chances of a restoration were hampered by the prospective king's insistence that the tricolour flag be replaced by the white flag of the Bourbons. In the hopes of resolving this problem, the monarchists took their time in preparing the 'Constitution of 1875', while the word 'republic' only appeared in the legislation as the result of an amendment (passed by 353 votes to 352) in the law relating to the appointment of a president. The first president, Marshal MacMahon, the duke of Magenta, was a conservative and ardent Catholic. MacMahon was happy when he could choose a royalist, such as the duke de Broglie, as his prime minister, but the increasing strength of the republicans in the Chamber of Deputies began to make this difficult. A serious clash developed in the summer of 1877. MacMahon dismissed a republican government which had a majority in the chamber and sought to replace it with a ministry under de Broglie. When the chamber passed a vote of no confidence in de Broglie, the chamber was dismissed and a new election was held. The government was determined to secure a majority favourable to de Broglie and MacMahon, and failed. An attempt to impose another ministry like that of de Broglie also failed, and MacMahon bowed to the will of the chamber by appointing a republican ministry. The significance of these events being that it was no longer possible for the president to choose a ministry without the agreement of a majority in the chamber. Early in 1879, with eighteen months of his term of office still to run, MacMahon resigned; with him went the 'republic of the dukes'.

In Germany the elected chamber of the imperial *Reichstag* never acquired such power. The deputies here, Anderson (p.111) writes 'offered ... no effective challenge to the forces of autocracy and of military and bureaucratic conservatism which dominated the new empire'. Perhaps German politicians, especially Liberal politicians, can be criticized for failing to check the power of the Kaiser and his ministers; and such criticism has been common with historians who, with the benefit of hindsight, have traced the unfortunate route followed by German politics in the first half of the twentieth century. Yet it is also important to understand the context of the politics of Imperial Germany. It was a federation of different states, and different regional traditions could have an impact on voting patterns. Religion also had a bearing on the way that politics were shaped in the early years of the empire. There were about 40 million Protestants, 24 million Catholics and about a million following other beliefs in the empire. There was no tradition of aggressive anti-clericalism, but the conservatism of Pius IX and his various declarations during the 1860s and early 1870s led the Liberals into an alliance with Bismarck and forced the naturally conservative Catholic Centre Party into opposition. The Curias' refusal to acknowledge a German envoy to the Vatican in 1872 and the Archbishop of Cologne's attempt to enforce papal infallibility on theologians at the University of Bonn, who because of their teaching positions were Prussian civil servants, saw the opening of the *Kulturkampf* (which could roughly be translated in this context as 'ideological struggle' though the literal translation 'struggle for culture' betrays the liberal view that ultimately Catholicism lacked culture) directed against the Church. Concerned Liberals appear to have pressed Bismarck into going further than he had initially intended. This meant that one of the most efficient political groupings on the right, the Centre Party, was labelled as *Reichsfeinde* ('enemies of the empire') by Bismarck in the early 1870s; while the more natural critics of the system, the Liberals, were linked with it and supported the repressive legislation of the *Kulturkampf*. Towards the end of the decade, shrewd politician that he was, Bismarck allowed elements of the *Kulturkampf legislation* to be relaxed so as to bring the Centre Party over to his side in his new struggle against the socialists. The Centre Party, accordingly, supported his economic and social legislation.

The economic and social reform legislation from above was also a means of appealing to the educated middle classes who might, otherwise have supported a more critical form of Liberalism. The men in this social group benefited from opportunities for social advancement within the state bureaucracy; another reason for them backing the existing order.

It is also worth noting the importance of ideology rather than pragmatism in German politics. This may, of course, have been as much an effect as a cause of the 'failure' of politicians. Nevertheless, to quote one constitutional historian of Germany:

> Many contemporaries and critics, past and present, have pointed at the unique character of German political parties, compared with the political parties of other European states. This applies particularly to the extent to which principles, doctrines and ideas, indeed ideologism played a role in them … Even debates on purely practical issues such as protective tariffs were discussed by German parliamentarians on ideological, even metaphysical, premises. (Koch, 1984, p.135)

German Liberals were more concerned with the principle of the legal accountability of ministers than with parliamentary accountability. The *Rechtsstaat*, the principal of legal accountability of the state bureaucracy, was finally achieved in Prussia in the 1870s. There is some justification for saying that, since the system was working, since the economy was growing and since progressive reforms were being satisfactorily introduced from above, the Liberals, and the middle class in general in Germany, had a state functioning in their interests. Moreover they could look with some satisfaction at French constitutional forms which had brought defeat in war and then the Commune, and the British parliamentary system which had witnessed another round of popular disorder urging parliamentary reform in 1866–7.

I want to turn now to the differences which Anderson stresses with reference to Austria-Hungary and Russia. After the *Ausgleich* of 1867 (Anderson, p.104) there were two parliaments in Austria-Hungary. That in Hungary was dominated by the Magyars, and determined to maintain their authority in the kingdom. The *Reichsrat* in the western half of the empire was initially structured to ensure a German majority; something which generated hostility from the other nationalities, particularly the Czechs who aspired to an autonomy akin to that of the Magyars. To ensure the *Reichsrat's* agreement to the 1867 compromise, the monarchy promised individual rights and an independent judiciary; but it never yielded any of its power over the appointment and dismissal of ministers to the deputies. Moreover when at the close of the nineteenth and beginning of the twentieth centuries, the empire toyed with universal manhood suffrage, it was as a ploy to undermine nationalist parties and maintain the existing structure.

The Russian Empire maintained its autocratic nature even more fiercely. The tsar's authority was identified as coming from God. During the reign of Nicholas I a catechism used in churches and schools urged obedience and quietism as follows:

> Response: God commands us to love and obey from the inmost recesses of the heart every authority, and particularly the Emperor.
>
> Question: What examples confirm this doctrine?
>
> Response: The example of Jesus Christ himself, who lived and died in allegiance to the Emperor of Rome, and respectfully submitted to the judgement which condemned him to death ... (quoted in Westwood, 1987, p.16)

The Fundamental Laws of Imperial Russia, which were issued in the year after the Revolution of 1905 as a direct result of that revolution, put the empire on the road to constitutionalism. Even so, at the outset, they described the tsar's position in terms very different from that employed in other constitutions. 'The All-Russian Emperor possesses the supreme autocratic power. Not only fear and conscience, but God himself, commands obedience to his authority.' Before listing the rights of the citizen to assembly, conscience and property, the laws explained: 'The defence of the Throne and of the Fatherland is a sacred obligation of every Russian subject' (quotations in Dmytryshyn, 1974, pp.387 and 389).

Finally, it is worth highlighting a general trend. During the nineteenth century there was an increasing amount of legislation as states across Europe took on various social and economic tasks. In consequence, while the parliaments which debated this legislation may not have had sovereign power, their role did have the effect of increasing their visibility and enhancing their power and authority.

Laws, citizens and subjects

The constitutions which we have been looking at provided broad statements of how a particular state was to be organized, and of the rights and duties of its citizens, or the subjects of its monarch. Laws passed by the states legislatures, or decrees issued by its executive subsequently describe, more specifically, what individuals can and cannot, must and must not do, and define citizens/subjects in relation to the state – as conscripts, criminals, jurors, taxpayers, voters – and in relation to each other – employer–employee, husband–wife, master–servant, parent/guardian–child. The constitutions of nineteenth-century Europe increasingly promised freedom from arbitrary action and equality before the law, but how did this work in practice? I want to explore this now under three headings:

1   employers and workers

2   rural workers and peasants

3   men and women.

Employers and workers

Exercise   Read Document I.13 and answer the following questions:

1   What would be the modern word for the kind of organization which Le Chapelier is condemning?

2   What does he consider ought to exist in place of such organizations?

Specimen Answers   1   Trade unions.

2   Personal bargaining between master and man. (The term 'master and man' was the one invariably used in reference to artisan trade in the eighteenth and early nineteenth century.)

This speech by Isaac Réné Le Chapelier (1754–94) introduced a law which was to remain in existence in France until March 1884. The Le Chapelier Law has been criticized by labour activists in France and by many historians of the French working class as the principal instrument for the repression of workers' organizations during most of the nineteenth century. But look carefully at what Le Chapelier said; he believed that workers' wages were too low, and that French workers were not as well paid as their English counterparts. The danger that he saw was from alternative organizations coming between the individual and the nation. Corporations could be seen as running counter to the third clause of the Declaration of the Rights of Man and Citizen which forbade any authority to any individual or organization if this did not emanate directly from the nation. Corporations were therefore 'counter-revolutionary' as only the nation could guarantee an individual's rights.

The Le Chapelier Law also forbade coalitions of employers; these too were counter-revolutionary. But, as the law was subsequently enforced, these were never dealt with as strictly. Moreover subsequent legislation put the worker at an even greater disadvantage. From 1803 all French workmen (as women were excluded from this legislation) were required to carry a workbook, the *livret ouvrier*. This was to contain details of a man's employment history and had to be made up by an employer when a man left his employ. While the book did not contain comments on the man's behaviour, any working man found by the police without his *livret* was liable to six months' imprisonment as a vagabond. The *livret* continued to be a requirement until 1890. In a variety of other respects too, for much of the nineteenth century, the law favoured the employer over the employee. The *conseils de prud hommes*, established in 1808 to resolve small conflicts between employers and employees, had a majority of the former; and breach of contract was a criminal offence for a workman, but an employer could only be pursued under the civil code. This latter might be rationalized in as much as, if a worker was fined, he could be unable to pay the fine; but if an employer was imprisoned, his time away from his business, or the stigma of imprisonment, could lead to its collapse.

Such legislation never prevented workers' organizations, and union activity was conducted under the guise of mutual aid societies established to provide sickness, retirement or death benefits, and the closed trade organizations known as *campagnonages*. The latter were in decline by the middle of the century, and the kind of organization which we would recognize as trades unions were appearing by the last quarter, but they, and their members, were rarely on an equal footing with the employers before the law. Indeed many union activists spurned the latter and favoured an aggressive and violent syndicalism (see Anderson, p.361).

Though they did not have their origins in an interpretation of the Declaration of the Rights of Man and Citizen, laws, in other countries of nineteenth-century Europe put the employee, and his self-help organizations, at a disadvantage.

In Britain, for example, at the beginning of the nineteenth century there were a variety of laws which hedged in trade union activity and put workers in an inferior position to their employers. The repeal of the Combination Acts in 1824 gave some toleration to unions organized for collective bargaining over hours and wages, but the Master and Servant Act of 1823 made the worker liable in criminal law for breach of contract, while the employer could only be proceeded against by a civil suit. It was not until the last third of the century that greater equality was established between 'master' and 'servant' (1867 and 1875), that union funds were given protection (1871), that peaceful picketing was tolerated, and that the threat of prosecution for strike activity under the Common Law notion of 'restraint of trade' was removed (1875).

In Germany many state governments passed a succession of laws around the beginning of the century restricting union activity and relegating the worker, more effectively, to a subservient position. Laws such as the Prussian *Gewerbeordnung* of 1845 prohibited combinations by masters as well as by workmen. This law was temporarily set aside during the Revolution of 1848, but was in use against workers in the following year. Legislation giving greater toleration to trade unions in Germany, like the *Gewerbeordnung* of the North German Confederation of 1869, tended to precede the growth of large unions, rather than vice-versa as in Britain. It was the product of economic liberalism rather than workers' action. The economic boom of the late 1860s and early 1870s generated a growth of unions in Germany and a wave of strike action, but rather than reverse what was regarded as progressive economic legislation, the government of the Empire opted increasingly to use the laws against political associations to investigate union activities and to check union power.

Rural workers and peasants

For most of the nineteenth century it was workers from the skilled trades who were unionized. Unskilled workers, most notably the dockers, began to get organized in Britain during the 1880s. But the largest single section of the workforce across Europe throughout the nineteenth century was engaged in agriculture. In Britain, where this section of the workforce was most clearly decreasing, the rural worker was primarily a wage labourer well before the nineteenth century; but this was not the case elsewhere. During the eighteenth century continental Europe had witnessed a feudal revival with lords seeking to maximize the profits from their lands and putting pressure on the peasants who owed them a variety of dues and services in labour, cash, or kind. The French Revolution abolished resurgent feudalism in France. Eighteenth-century monarchs had been seeking to limit the power of their nobles and improve the overall agricultural production of their lands by reforming the feudal system; the example of the French Revolution often encouraged this policy, and in many places where it did not, French bayonets achieved what example could not. Central to the abolition of the vestiges of feudalism, was the emancipation of the peasantry.

Emancipation, however, did not ensure personal freedom for every peasant, nor did it mean an equality of rights between peasant and lord. In Baden, Prussia and Bavaria, for example, initial emancipation decrees appeared respectively in 1783, 1807 and 1808, but in each case it was not until the revolutions of 1848 that all servile obligations on the part of the peasants and all privileges on the part of the lords were removed. Moreover the hired hand, who lived in the home or on the holding of the lord generally remained in an inferior position. It was not until the end of the First World War that the Prussian Junkers' right of punishment of the unmarried men living on his lands was removed. In Russia emancipation came in 1861; but it was not until the scare given the autocracy by the Revolution of 1905, that a peasant was permitted to travel and settle anywhere in the empire, to set up as a private landowner with a consolidated, independent holding, and to be tried only for offences defined as crimes by the general criminal code.

This, in turn, raises a crucial point about citizenship in much of continental Europe during the nineteenth century, particularly in the east and the south. Citizenship here was much less concerned with political equality and much more with legal equality; for the peasant, the end of feudalism and his right to property were more important than the right to vote. In 1848–9 peasants commonly sided with those who appeared the most opposed to the vestiges of feudalism and serfdom; in Silesia this was the democrats, in Hungary it was the nationalist nobility, in Habsburg Galicia it was the Austrian Emperor. The end of feudal structures meant changes in the legal title of land. Some peasants acquired land as a direct result of emancipation, and a few were able to purchase it. But as land increasingly became a marketable commodity, so common land began to be enclosed and converted into freeholds or leaseholds. Again a few peasants could profit from this and purchase such land, but many more, who relied on common land for forage and fuel and for grazing an animal or two, found themselves seriously disadvantaged. In some instances emancipation served ultimately to force peasants in many areas into the ranks of landless, and often disgruntled, labourers.

Men and women

Exercise   Read Document I.14. Might it be argued that these regulations establish formal inequality? and if so why?

Discussion   I think you could argue that these regulations establish a kind of formal inequality for example, the Civil Code only authorizes men to sign official documents, and puts the wife as the subordinate in a marriage.

This also brings us back to Hazel Mill's comments on the significance of the Declaration of the Rights of Man and Citizen in Video 1 (pp.672–744).

Women's inequality was further underlined by rulings in jurisprudence and, for example, by the Criminal Code of 1810 which authorized the penalty of imprisonment from three months to two years for a wife convicted of adultery, while a husband, guilty of the same offence, was only liable to a fine. France was not alone in such regulations. Across nineteenth-century Europe arguments were put forward that the fundamental differences between men and women necessitated separate spheres of action in the world. The man was the dominant, superior being whose task, among others, was to protect the woman. The woman – 'the weaker vessel' – did not have the attributes for public life. She was more emotional, less able to cope with education, but was designed to bear children and run the household. This ideology was used to justify the husband taking control of the wife's property, and even wife-beating. Moreover, in the words of Lord Cranworth during a debate on divorce in the House of Lords in 1850, it was acceptable for the husband to be 'a little profligate', but not for the wife, since she might use this as a means of 'passing spurious offspring upon the husband'.

Of course there were opponents to this perception of the order of things, and feminists were not just to be found among women. In *The Duties of Man* Giuseppe Mazzini urged his male readers:

> Blot out your mind any idea of superiority [over women]; you have none whatever. The prejudice of ages has created through unequal education and the perennial oppression of the laws that *apparent* intellectual inferiority which you use today as an argument for maintaining the oppression. (Mazzini, 1860, p.62)

Feminism in France, in the late nineteenth century, found one of its most dynamic advocates in Léon Richer, a republican notary who began publishing the newspaper *Le Droit des Femmes* in 1869 and, the following year, organized the *Association pour le Droit des Femmes* both of which called for a revision of the Civil Code, a single moral standard, improved educational and job prospects for women.

The position of women was not static throughout the century. In Britain, for example, divorce was permitted in 1857, though on terms generally much tougher for the wife – she could be divorced for adultery, but she could only divorce her husband if his adultery was incestuous or otherwise sexually perverted; in 1870 the Married Woman's Property Act gave a wife greater control, and protection of her property; educational and employment opportunities for middle-class women increased piecemeal. But advance in one area could go hand-in-hand with greater disadvantages elsewhere. The Civil Code for the German Empire, first published in 1887 but not enacted until 1900, allowed single women to sign contracts, bring lawsuits, own property and to engage in commercial transactions on the same basis as men. It also abolished the laws which had allowed husbands to punish their wives physically. But, at the same time, it reinforced the husband's authority in a marriage giving him continuing control of his wife's property, though not her earnings, and making him the sole decision-maker over matters involving the children. With the exceptions of Finland (a precocious, semi-autonomous province of the Russian Empire) in 1906 and Norway in 1907, no state in Europe on the eve of the First World War had conceded that women had any right to suffrage.

Interpretations

How have historians interpreted the material discussed in this unit? How should you interpret it?

It is common for such issues to be discussed generally in the context of a single state, though with acknowledgements to events elsewhere particularly if they can be seen to have had an influence on the state under discussion, or if they provide a significant contrast. Thus the traditional historians of English constitutional development tended to take a self congratulatory line, noting that there were no revolutions in nineteenth-century Britain, but rather a steady constitutional progress, a model for less fortunate countries. This is not a view which finds much favour today, though in some respects it has been the interpretation of the ideal nineteenth-century liberal state taken up by some historians of Germany to contrast with that country's *Sonderweg* (special way). The 'failure' of the German bourgeoisie to carry out a bourgeois revolution, of some sort, and their decision to side with an authoritarian, military state, led to war in 1914 and, worse still, to the Nazi seizure of power in 1933. There is an echo of this, perhaps, in Anderson's criticism of the German Liberals' 'failures' during the *Kaiserreich* which I have discussed above (pp.28–9).

Yet when we look comparatively at the different states of Europe it is possible to argue that there are remarkable similarities in the way that they were developing. Constitutions and parliamentary systems were becoming more and more common in the states of Europe over the nineteenth century. Parliaments were wielding more and more influence even, if with difficulty, in the autocratic empires of the east. Furthermore where progress was very slow, notably in the case of women and labour, there were similarities. Feminist historians have little difficulty in demonstrating that the nation state of the nineteenth century essentially enshrined, in both its constitution and its laws, a patriarchal view of society. While Marxist historians, and others, have long argued that these states worked in favour of bourgeois and capitalist interests, restricting the working classes and their organizations. The problem in both of these cases is explaining why this happened. Was it a conspiracy on the part of male, bourgeois capitalists?; and if so, exactly how did such a conspiracy work? Was it a rationalization, through the law, of the way that things had always been accepted and understood, driven more by inertia and/or traditional assumption that women and workers were inferior?; and if it was this, how might such a conclusion be supported?

References

Anderson, B. C. (1991), 'State building and bureaucracy in early nineteenth-century Germany', *Central European History*, 22, pp.222–47.

Church, C. H. (1983), *Europe in 1830*, Allen and Unwin, London.

Clark, M. (1984), *Modern Italy, 1871–1982*, Longman, London.

Dmytryshyn, B. (ed.) (1974), *Imperial Russia: A Source Book, 1700–1917*, 2nd edn, The Dryden Press, Hinsdale, Illinois.

Gash, N. (1972), *Sir Robert Peel*, Longman, London.

Hinsley, F.H. (1963), *Power and the Pursuit of Peace: Theory and Practice in the History of Relations between States*, Cambridge University Press, Cambridge.

Koch, H.W. (1984), *A Constitutional History of Germany in the Nineteenth and Twentieth Centuries*, Longman, London.

Mazzini, G. (1860), *The Duties of Man*, J.M. Dent, London; reprinted 1907.

Roberts, J.M. (1974), *The Mythology of the Secret Societies*, 2nd edn, Paladin, St Albans.

Sahlins, P. (1989), *Boundaries. The Making of France and Spain in the Pyrenees*, University of California Press, Berkeley, Cal.

Westwood, J.N. (1987), *Endurance and Endeavour: Russian History 1812–1986*, 3rd edn, Oxford University Press, Oxford.

Unit 3
Bureaucracy

Prepared for the course team by Richard Bessel

Contents

Study timetable

Weeks of Study	Texts	Video	AC
2	Unit 3; Offprints 2, 3; Anderson		

Aim

The aim of this unit is to help you to understand the development of bureaucracy in nineteenth-century Europe, something which should come in handy when this topic appears on the list of TMA questions or on the Exam paper.

Objectives

The objectives of this unit are to encourage you to think about and be equipped to discuss:

1   the origins of the modern bureaucratic state;

2   why and how state bureaucracies altered and expanded in Europe during the nineteenth century;

3   how European state bureaucracies acted;

4   interpretative frameworks for assessing the role and functions of state bureaucracy.

These are themes with not only historical relevance. An understanding of these topics involves not only learning about the Napoleonic state or the Prussian reform programmes of Stein and Hardenberg; it also means understanding the roots of the modern world which we inhabit (and in which we constantly are confronted by state bureaucracies as a matter of course).

Freedom depends far more on the administration than on the constitution. (Barthold Georg Niebuhr, 1815; quoted in Koselleck, 1989, p.217)

In order to take part in public life, one must be a salaried and dependent servant of the state, one must belong completely to the bureaucratic caste. (Otto von Bismarck, 1838; quoted in Sheehan, 1989, p.433)

Introduction

A few years ago the historian Michael Geyer, while introducing an article about 'The state in National Socialist Germany', noted a fascinating and significant paradox. He wrote:

> It is curious, indeed, that the nineteenth century, which did not know strong states, ultimately may turn out to be the century of the state, if only because the state formed a coherent unit. (Geyer, 1984, p.193)

Geyer was writing about one of the most incoherent and most expansive twentieth-century states, and he was commenting upon the inadequacy of nineteenth-century concepts of the state (as 'a coherent unit') as tools for understanding the nature of twentieth-century states. In making this observation, he offered an important statement about the nature of the state both in the nineteenth century and the twentieth. Our conceptions of the state and of bureaucracy remain essentially derivative of the ideal-typical nineteenth-century European state and state bureaucracy. Accordingly, they tend to assume a coherent bureaucratic domination governed by a set of rational rules – essentially the model presented by Max Weber, who described bureaucracy and state structures as he had seen them develop in Europe during the late nineteenth and early twentieth centuries.

For the purposes of this course, we need to approach the subject of bureaucracies and state structures from the opposite direction of that taken by Geyer. Our task is to understand the nature and importance of state bureaucracy in nineteenth-century Europe against the background of our familiarity with something rather different – both vastly larger and less coherent – in the twentieth. Our vantage point – looking back over two centuries during which there has been an increasing bureaucratization of European societies – is radically different from the vantage point of nineteenth-century Europeans. Many things which may seem self-evident to us and give the twentieth-century (European) state its strength – for example, that the state's servants should administer fairly a system of welfare payments for the unemployed, the disabled etc., regulate traffic, inspect factories and restaurants, set and enforce building and housing standards, and assign to each of us a tax inspector – were not part of the lives of Europeans at the outset of the nineteenth century. State bureaucracy meant essentially the small but growing administrative apparatuses of government – whose main task was extracting revenues from the state's subjects – and, of course, armies. By late twentieth-century standards, the nineteenth-century European state may have been relatively coherent, but it also was relatively limited and, in that sense, relatively weak.

Of course, the nineteenth-century European state has a pre-history as well as a post-history; the European state is not something which appeared suddenly after 1789. Eighteenth-century Europe contained very strong absolutist states. However, these states did not possess bureaucracies in the modern sense. Their officials, the numbers of whom often were not inconsiderable (although the state's servants were not properly counted until the nineteenth century), tended to acquire office by inheriting it, being granted it by patronage or by purchasing it; remuneration tended either to be non-existent (where officials performed duties which flowed from their social rank) or by the fruits of office (e.g. the acceptance of fees for services performed). This system of receiving reward by taking the fruits of office, of 'venal' office-holding, looks to our modern eyes like corruption, but this perception is perhaps a reflection of our acceptance of the concept of bureaucracy as expounded by Max Weber. (Weber's definition of bureaucracy and the theme of corruption are both discussed below.)

As Michael Mann (1993) notes in the second volume of his monumental comparative study, *The Sources of Social Power*, in the middle of the eighteenth century 'states were not remotely bureaucratic' in the modern sense of the term. By the end of 'the long nineteenth century' this had changed profoundly:

> By 1914, almost all central, and most local-regional, officials received salaries. Office owning by hereditary right or purchase had virtually disappeared. Only part-time honorific office holding survived in large numbers at the local level. (Mann, 1993, p.472)

That is to say, the office belonged not to the office-holder, but to the state. Bureaucracies also increasingly came to be divided by function and subordinated to a centralized hierarchy (rather than officials simply being in charge of a particular geographic area, largely free from control from above), and to a greater or lesser extent appointment and promotion came to be dependent upon an impersonal measurement of competence. Thus, by the eve of the First World War – at least in the developed western European countries of Britain, France and Germany – government bureaucracies had assumed the basic form which we expect of them today, even though their size and the range of their concerns was very limited by late twentieth-century standards.

The growth of state bureaucracies in the nineteenth century occurred against the background of substantial economic expansion. This meant that, while European state bureaucracies expanded considerably in the nineteenth century, generally speaking 'state activities *decreased* as a proportion of national economic activity between the mid-eighteenth and the early twentieth century' (Mann, 1993, p.368). Indeed, there are examples of European states getting out of the administration of important sectors of the economy: in the German states – most notably in Prussia – during the second half of the nineteenth century the state largely ceased to manage the coal and iron mines which it had run heretofore. Of course, comparisons drawn between European states' activities in the early nineteenth century and their activities at its end are also in large measure a reflection of the fact that the century began with the Napoleonic wars and ended relatively peacefully, until the great conflagration of the First World War. State expenditures were, and are still, in considerable measure expenditures on and by the military (also an important bureaucracy!). The state's role in the economy necessarily expands in wartime; and the fact that it did not expand more than actually was the case in the nineteenth century is due to the fact that (at least in comparison with the eighteenth and twentieth centuries) the nineteenth century was relatively peaceful in Europe.

Weber and bureaucracy

Before we proceed to examine the structures and practices of nineteenth-century European states and their bureaucracies, we first should review the framework within which these structures and practices commonly are discussed (a framework to which we already have alluded to above): that presented by the 'great bourgeois antipode of Karl Marx' (Mommsen, 1974, p.47), the German sociologist Max Weber (whom you encounter repeatedly in this course).

In his great work *Economy and Society*, first published in 1922 (shortly after his sudden death in 1920), Weber presented his famous ideal-typical theory of 'three pure types of legitimate domination (*Herrschaft*)'. (Note: The German term 'Herrschaft' is translated by Guenther Roth and Claus Wittich, in the English translation of *Economy and Society* used below, alternatively as 'domination' and 'authority'; please be aware that in Weber the two English terms are actually one and the same.) In his book, Weber classified the claims made by rulers to legitimate their rule: 'rational grounds' (i.e. 'legal authority'), 'traditional grounds' ('traditional authority'), and 'charismatic grounds' ('charismatic authority'). For the purposes of our discussion here it is the first of these, 'legal authority', which is most important (although, of course, it is quite possible to have a 'charismatic' ruler who uses a bureaucracy to implement his commands), and Weber's classification has provided the basic yardstick against which 'bureaucracy' is measured:

> The purest type of exercise of legal authority is that which employs a bureaucratic administrative staff. Only the supreme chief of the organization occupies his position of dominance (*Herrenstellung*) by virtue of appropriation, of election, or of having been designated for the succession. But even *his* authority consists in a sphere of legal 'competence'. The whole administrative staff under the supreme authority then consists, in the purest type, of individual officials ... who are appointed and function according to the following criteria:
>
> 1   They are personally free and subject to authority only with respect to their impersonal obligations.
>
> 2   They are organized in a clearly defined hierarchy of offices.
>
> 3   Each office has a clearly defined sphere of competence in the legal sense.
>
> 4   The office is filled by a free contractual relationship. Thus, in principle, there is free selection.
>
> 5   Candidates are selected on the basis of technical qualifications. In the most rational case, this is tested by examination or guaranteed by diplomas certifying technical training, or both. They are *appointed*, not elected.

6   They are remunerated by fixed salaries in money, for the most part with a right to pensions. Only under certain circumstances does the employing authority, especially in private organizations, have a right to terminate the appointment, but the official is always free to resign...

7   The office is treated as the sole, or at least the primary, occupation of the incumbent.

8   It constitutes a career. There is a system of 'promotion' according to seniority or to achievement, or both. Promotion is dependent on the judgement of superiors.

9   The official works entirely separated from ownership of the means of administration and without appropriation of his position.

10   He is subject to strict and systematic discipline and control in the conduct of his office. (Weber, 1978, vol. i, pp.220–1. See also Mommsen, 1974, esp. pp.72–94.)

This is the 'ideal-typical' model of 'bureaucracy', which 'once fully established is among those social structures which are hardest to destroy' (Weber, 1978, vol.ii, p.987). As Weber went on to make clear, this model is not exclusive to *state* bureaucracies: 'It may be applied in profit-making business or in charitable organizations, or in any number of other types of private enterprises serving ideal or material ends.' However, here we are concerned with it primarily in relation to state bureaucracies, particularly as they developed in the century or so before Weber sat down to describe them. Weber's is not really a description of the actual workings of any specific state structure, but rather a distillation of the principles which define how a state structure *ought* to work. The working principles outlined by Weber took shape within and, to a greater or lesser extent, were applied to organizations which formed the backbone of the state as 'a coherent unit' in nineteenth-century Europe.

The French model

The obvious place to begin an examination of bureaucracy in nineteenth-century Europe is revolutionary France, which gave the world its first modern state bureaucracy. *Ancien regime* France certainly had large numbers of people employed, either directly or indirectly, by the state, but not in what we would describe as a modern bureaucracy. Most of these state servants were *officiers*, who owned their office (which usually they had bought); only a minority were salaried working employees (*commissaires*), and the latter were usually subordinate to the former. The Revolution of 1789 brought truly revolutionary change: office venality was abolished; the bureaucracy (and now it is possible to use the word) became salaried; the state was committed to rational principles of hierarchy and function and to centralization (Mann, 1993, p.460). Despite the initial intentions of the revolutionaries, the numbers of salaried state servants grew substantially, as political terror and war – with the need to supply armies, provision cities, root out counter-revolutionaries – meant that the size of the new state rivalled that of the old. In 1793 the numerical strength of the French bureaucracy as a whole – at 250,000 – was probably five times that of the pre-Revolutionary salaried administration in 1788 (although, if one were to include *all* the officials of the *ancien regime* the figures probably would be roughly comparable (see Church, 1981, p.72; Mann, 1993, p.461). What the revolutionary regime and the Directory (1795–9) added to the new bureaucracy was not so much an increase in size but, as Clive Church (1981, p. 143) has pointed out, 'a new dimension of hierarchy and speciali-zation, new ideas and rules of operation, and, above all, a career pattern leading to pensions, consistency, and performance'; thus, as Crane Brinton noted many years ago, the Napoleonic bureaucracy was largely in place before the advent of Napoleon.

Nevertheless, the importance of Napoleon in shaping and defining the modern state bureaucracy has been pointed out many times and cannot be ignored. Napoleon used the bureaucracy at his disposal, developed it in the context of a strong, centralized and hierarchical state, and spread it (and thus its structures and practices) throughout Europe. All in all, between 1789 and 1815 the outlines of a modern bureaucracy were created which provided a model ever since and which proved quite durable.

Exercise　　How far do you think the state bureaucracy which took shape in France between 1789 and 1815 corresponded to the model described by Max Weber?

Discussion　　To a considerable degree it did, at least on paper. The practice of buying office, which had prevailed under the *ancien regime*, had been abolished; remuneration by fees had been replaced by salaries; although patronage and family connections remained important, careers had come to depend upon impersonal criteria of competence. The goal was to create a profes-sional state bureaucracy which was dedicated to public service – whose members would serve the state rather than themselves.

Certainly if one can speak, as Clive Church does, of a bureaucracy characterized by 'hierarchy and specialization, new ideas and rules of operation, and, above all, a career pattern leading to pensions, con-sistency, and performance', then one is speaking in terms consonant with Weber's ideal-typical description. The question, of course, is to what extent the practice conformed to the theory. The actual reach of the revolu-tionary bureaucracy remained limited. (Michael Mann (1993, p.461) asks rhetorically of the French revolutionary bureaucracy: 'Can a fiscal administration be called bureaucratic if it manages to collect 10 per cent of the taxes it demands?'.) The repeated regime changes in France – the Directory, Napoleon's coup, the falls of Napoleon in 1814 and 1815 and subsequent Bourbon Restoration, as well as the later regime changes in 1830 and 1848 were accompanied by purges of the bureaucracy and deep incursions of party politics into the workings of the civil service. As Roger Magraw (1983, p.167) noted, writing about the Bonapartist state of Louis Napoleon in the 1850s and 1860s, 'the ideal of a neutral bureaucracy above class interests ... was always unattainable'.

We need therefore to be a bit careful before assuming that the machinery of a country in which no regime lasted longer than two decades during the first two-thirds of the nineteenth century could be filled by bureaucrats who (in Weber's words) really were 'personally free and subject to authority only with respect to their impersonal obligations'.

Nevertheless, the French state bureaucracy remained numerous and powerful throughout the nineteenth century – under royalist, imperial and republican constitutions. In the 1860s, the French state's servants roughly numbered 265,000 (alongside 360,000 soldiers and 24,000 gendarmes) (Magraw, 1983, p.167). On the eve of the First World War there were about a half a million civil servants in France, and employment in the expanding civil service proved increasingly attractive to wider circles of citizens. Working as a government bureaucrat was safer than careers in industry or the independent professions, where the vagaries of the economic cycle often spelled ruin; at least in the higher ranks, the civil service offered high salaries; the spread of education meant that more people were able to obtain the qualifications necessary for civil-service employment; and employment in the state bureaucracy provided many people with good opportunities for social advancement, especially under Republican government during the last third of the century (Zeldin, 1973, p.114). These advantages were, of course, not exclusive to France.

Bureaucracy in Prussia and Germany

No less important than revolutionary France in giving the modern state bureaucracy its ideal form were Prussia and Germany during the nineteenth century. In 1911 the historian Otto Hintze observed, in an oft-quoted phrase, that 'Germany is the classic land of the civil service in the European world' (Hintze, 1981, p.44). Like Weber, Hintze regarded the German civil service as a model, as the best in the world. The Prussian/German bureaucracy which so inspired Hintze and many others was in large measure a product of the Prussian reforms at the outset of the nineteenth century. Here too Napoleon played a key role: Prussia's defeat by the French Emperor in 1806 and the Peace of Tilsit of 1807 – which halved the size of the kingdom, saddled it with large war reparations, and forced it to accept the presence of French troops on its soil – compelled the Prussians to make radical reforms in the way the kingdom was administered, in order to bring about its return to great-power status. Faced with disaster and the urgent need to improve the financial efficacy of the Prussian state, forced to admit the bankruptcy of their policies and mode of governance, and determined to catch up with France and Britain, Prussia's rulers aimed to modernize economy, society and the state.

　　What were the Prussian reforms, and what were their consequences for the development of the state bureaucracy? The reforms, associated with the names of Karl Freiherr von Stein (who was named the Prussian king's chief minister in October 1807 and forced from office a year later as a result of French pressure) and Karl August von Hardenberg (who served as

Staatskanzler – i.e. in effect Prussia's first prime minister – from June 1810 until his death in 1822), were a fundamental step towards the modernization of state and society in nineteenth-century Europe. Central to Stein's reform programme was the reorganization of government, in order (as James Sheehan (1989, p.299) has put it) to turn 'the state into an effective instrument for social change' – for social emancipation and economic development. This was the goal of the famous 'October Edict' of 1807 ('On the Facilitation of Property Ownership, the Free Use of Land, and the Personal Condition of Peasants'), and various measures which followed over the next few years. Prussians and their commercial activity were to be subjected to the 'rule of law' (*Rechtsstaat*); restrictions on the buying of noble estates were removed; and all occupations were opened to both nobles and commoners. In short, Prussia was to become what we recognize as a modern society with a modern state (although, it must be noted, the influence of the old nobility and the importance of the old established hierarchies in fact proved quite durable).

For Stein, reshaping the state bureaucracy was essential (conditioned no doubt by the fact that he himself had had a long career in the Prussian bureaucracy). For our purposes here, it is the reform of the bureaucracy which Stein set in motion, which provides the main focus. These changes are alluded to, unfortunately only in passing, by Anderson in your set text, where (on p.68) he mentions the Prussian government's introduction in 1809 of a system of examination for candidates for official posts. This may be seen as a step towards opening the civil service to those beyond the preserve of the old nobility and making it a 'career open to talent'; however, the three-stage examination system which had to be passed before one could enter state service also served to prevent 'outsiders' from climbing up this career ladder. No less important than the new examination system was the introduction of lifetime employment: civil servants no longer could be dismissed arbitrarily at any time; they could be transferred, but as members of the professional civil service (*Berufsbeamtentum*) they were employed for life. In return, they were expected to maintain their loyalty to the state at all times, as an expression of their dedication to the common good rather than due to fear of dismissal. These changes were part of a larger project to replace the old monarchical cabinet government with a more impersonal system in which, theoretically, policy was guided by the general interest – in which, as Hans Rosenberg (1966, p.208) put it, 'government was a matter of issues rather than personalities'.

At this point, you should turn to Offprint 3. In this article Rosenberg neatly puts the reform of the Prussian bureaucracy into context, and begins by relating it (as it must be related) to prior developments in France (discussed in schematic form above). He then presents a powerful argument about the significance of the reforms, in creating the basis of the 'bureaucratic absolutism' which replaced the old, discredited monarchical absolutism of the eighteenth century. Rosenberg's work on this subject was path breaking, with regard both to what he had to say about the development of bureaucracy in the nineteenth century and Prussia's role in the development and to the implications of his interpretation for the subsequent (destructive) history and historiography of Germany.

Exercise   Please read Offprint 3 now. What, in Rosenberg's view, were the main principles of the Prussian reform?

Discussion   Rosenberg points out that the aim of the Prussian reform was to create a bureaucracy which stood at the disposal of the government, ready to do its bidding independent of all social and economic factors; it incorporated three main organizational principles.

1   The 'nationalization' of local administration (by which the special rights and privileges of local governments were abrogated and replaced by a centralized, hierarchical state administration which applied administrative norms uniformly through the kingdom).

2   The replacement of administration organized along territorial lines (e.g. a ministry or department to administer, say, the province of Silesia) by administration organized according to specific areas of competence – by which the central administration, following the French model, was divided into the five 'classic' ministries: Foreign Affairs, War, Finance, Justice and Internal Affairs. (This occurred in Prussia and Württemberg in 1808, in Austria not until 1848.)

3   The replacement of the collegial principle of decision-making with bureaucratic decision-making along the lines of Napoleon's Prefects, whereby at each level of administration a single person was responsible for carrying out policy (i.e. a model which was essentially military) (Wunder, 1986, pp.24–5). (However, it should be noted that collegial forms of administration continued to operate at the regional – *Regierungsbezirk* – level in Prussia.)

These reforms essentially supplanted the self-administration of the nobility with a centralized, hierarchical bureaucracy whose task was to carry out government policy as determined from the centre. Similar reforms were implemented in the Prussian army (which had performed so disastrously against Napoleon's forces), where under Scharnhorst and Gneisenau regulations governing promotions, pay and pensions were standardized and the military bureaucracy was to a considerable extent 'liberated ... from the whims of personal interference by the monarch' (Rosenberg, 1966, p.216). The result, according to Rosenberg and other historians such as Hans-Ulrich Wehler, who have followed in Rosenberg's path, was the triumph of 'bureaucratic absolutism'. However, this does not necessarily mean that bureaucracy replaced monarchy as the real ruler in Prussia. Monarchs did matter, and it is possible to see the shift as somewhat less dramatic than Rosenberg did, that is, as a result of the reforms the king was now served by a different kind of administration.

The Prussian reforms were, of course, hardly 'democratic'. Prussian bureaucrats' own consciousness may have been framed by the oft-cited maxim, with which this unit opened, by Barthold Georg Niebuhr (a professor of Roman history at the University of Berlin, who regarded English local self-government as most closely approximating his ideal). However, while the reforms were designed to replace the old, discredited *Ständestaat* (state of estates), they were hardly designed to open the civil service to participation by the mass of the Prussian population. Quite the contrary. Employment in the higher reaches of the Prussian administrative bureaucracy was limited largely (and after 1817 completely) to university educated jurists with considerable financial means at their disposal. The question of a democratization of political power was taboo; commitment to economic liberalism went hand in hand with political repression; aristocratic privileges remained; the ownership of a Junker estate continued to provide the passport to careers in the upper reaches of the Prussian state; the Junkers retained control over the officer class.

It would be misleading to give the impression here that the Prussian experience equalled the 'German' experience – not only because 'Germany' did not yet exist. Indeed, it was the southern German states – Bavaria, Baden, Württemberg – which were in the vanguard in adopting constitutional government and anchoring the rights and privileges of their state bureaucrats in law. The most notable case was that of the south-west German state of Baden, which was both 'the most highly bureaucratized and the most genuinely constitutional German state' (Sheehan, 1989, p.426). The Baden constitution of August 1818, which not only had (like the Bavarian constitution decreed in May of that year) established a bicameral legislature (which in the Badenese case included a Chamber of Deputies elected by all those meeting the legal and economic qualifications of citizenship) but also guaranteed the special legal status of the bureaucracy. Flesh was put on the bones of this guarantee by the *Beamtenedikt* (civil-servants edict) of 1819, which established a privileged category of Badenese civil servants with job security and independence, set out rules for their appointment and promotion, and provided for training programmes and regular examinations. The result was, according to Sheehan (1989, p.427), 'to provide modes of recruitment and advancement that remained firmly in the hands of the bureaucrats themselves', – a remarkably modern set of procedures. Similarly, the Bavarian constitution of 1818 guaranteed state officials' social position (with an article on 'Conditions of Service and Pension Rights'), and the Württemberg constitution of 1819 granted job security and institutional autonomy to that kingdom's bureaucrats. Prussia caught up somewhat later, and in more piecemeal fashion, with what had been achieved by bureaucrats in the south-west German states.

Among the German states (and leaving such smaller states as the two Mecklenburgs out of the equation here) Austria remained an exception in this regard. In the wake of the Napoleonic Wars the Habsburg state aimed to reorganize its administration, integrate new territories and deal with its considerable financial problems without adopting constitutional government. Austria warded off constitutionalism and its bureaucracy, although an important political force, did not acquire the autonomy, the clear lines of authority or the consistent criteria for training and promotion enjoyed by its Badenese, Bavarian or Prussian counterparts. In Austria, the state remained the court until mid-century.

At the outset of the nineteenth century, the numbers of people employed as civil servants in the German states still were relatively small. Many functions which later would be organized by the state (e.g. transport, postal service) were still in private hands. In 1808, when the Prussian reforms were initiated, the number of Prussian civil servants in the narrow sense (i.e. not counting local officials or those employed in educational institutions) was roughly 23,000 (in a state with about nine million inhabitants and an army counting 235,000 men). (For these and the following figures, see Wunder, 1986, pp.44–50.) If one includes local officials whose duties and pay were determined by the Prussian state, the number was roughly 50,000. Indeed, there is no reason to assume that the bureaucratization described above must necessarily lead to the expansion of the state; in some ways the bureaucracy which replaced *ancien regime* officialdom actually interfered less in many areas of life, once many of the old privileges were abolished which fused economic and political functions.

Notwithstanding any shrinkage of the Prussian state in the immediate aftermath of the reforms, over the nineteenth century as a whole the size and functions of the bureaucracy grew. Education demanded an increasing amount of money and employed an increasing number of people: for example, Prussia at mid-century employed 29,000 teachers (Sheehan, 1989, p.435). Governments took an increasingly active interest in health and safety standards, employing public-health officials and factory inspectors, and passing legislation which, of course, had to be monitored and enforced. Perhaps by present-day standards the nineteenth century 'did not know strong states', but in general the state was getting stronger and state bureaucracies larger. By the end of the century, the numbers of people in German state employment were enormous. Consider the implications of the table below.

Table 1: State employees in the German Empire, 1875–1907

	Total State Employees	% in Education	% in Postal Service	% in Transport	% in Administration
1875	524,300	18.6%	15.4%	23.8%	41.8%
1881	647,855	17.8%	14.7%	32.7%	34.8%
1895	987,862	15.8%	18.3%	34.4%	32.5%
1907	1,475,312	13.5%	19.7%	38.6%	28.2%

Source: Wunder, 1986, p.72.

Before conclusions can be drawn from it, this table requires explanation. First, the German Empire was not the same as Prussia, and the figures given here refer to *all* state officials in the Empire (i.e. including those in the service of Prussia, Bavaria, etc.) and not just Imperial officials. Furthermore, the German civil service included many people whose counterparts were not civil servants in other countries (e.g. civil servants employed by the state railways and on local transport, and civil servants employed by the Reich Post Office), therefore their numbers cannot really be compared directly either with the numbers of Prussian civil servants at the outset of the century or with the rough figures given for France above (p.48). (State employees in transport and in the Post Office comprised more than half the total in 1895 and 1907 and formed the fastest growing categories of civil service employment. In 1913 some 205,741 German railway employees and 260,055 of the Reich postal employees (up from 78,000 in 1885) were civil servants (Wunder, 1986, p.82). Nevertheless, the basic trend shown here is clear: of a state bureaucracy growing rapidly in the context of an expanding industrial economy. Indeed (in contradistinction to the general trend identified by Michael Mann), in Germany the growth of state employment far outstripped the growth of population or the growth of the economy: between 1875 and 1907 Germany's population increased by roughly 41 per cent while the number of German civil servants increased by 182 per cent; in 1885 some 7.2 per cent of employees in Germany were classified as civil servants (*Staatsbedienstete*), and by 1907 this figure had risen to 10.6 per cent. It is also worth noting that, unlike at the outset of the nineteenth century, on the eve of the First World War, Germany's *civil* servants outnumbered by a considerable margin the 859,000 men serving in the army.

As in France, in Prussia/Germany public-sector employment held great attractions. Civil servants enjoyed secure employment immune to economic cycles, salaries which rose as they grew older (whereas workers' incomes usually declined as they aged and their strength waned), old-age pensions, housing allowances, and protection from dismissal. It also grew as government at all levels expanded to administer, regulate and control an increasingly complex industrial economy and society. Not only did the state grow at the centre, but local government grew as well and took on new functions which, of course, required more bureaucrats to carry them out. A good example is provided by developments which led to the growth of the municipal civil service in the city of Mannheim (in the south-west German state of Baden) from the last third of the nineteenth century. In 1869 a municipal slaughterhouse was built and in 1871 a municipal board of works (*Bauamt*) was established; from 1873 the gas works were run by the city; in 1874 the city began a street-cleaning service; in 1893 a professional fire-fighting service was established and in 1905 the electricity works were taken over by the city; and in 1905/6 the municipal transport system was extended and many of its employees given 'civil service' status (thus increasing the number of municipal civil servants by more than 50% at a stroke) (Wunder, 1986, pp.84–5).

The bureaucracy of the Russian Empire

Thus far we have focused on the classic examples of nineteenth-century bureaucracy in the more developed states of western and central Europe. Now let us consider a state whose practice may seem rather far removed from that of Napoleonic France or Reform Prussia: Tsarist Russia. Concluding their collection of essays on *Russian Officialdom: The Bureaucratization of Russian Society from the Seventeenth to the Twentieth Century*, Walter McKenzie Pintner and Dan Karl Rowney noted (in observations which neatly span the 'long nineteenth century' from 1789 to 1914–17):

> ... there seem to be two periods in which several strands end and new ones begin: (1) the last years of the eighteenth century and the early decades of the nineteenth, and (2) the early twentieth century, particularly the decade or two immediately following the Revolution of 1917.
>
> At the end of the eighteenth century the traditional importance of family ties, on the job training for civil service, and the mixed mili-

tary and civil career came to an end. These forms of socialization were replaced by a rapidly increasing emphasis on objective criteria, expressed in terms of the completion of specified periods of formal education prior to service, and a drastic reduction in the number of civil officials with prior military service. Civil service became a life-time career with its own specific entrance requirements.

The Revolution of 1917 ended the importance of noble birth and inherited wealth as factors affecting officialdom, but two threads at least span this early twentieth-century period of change. Under the new Bolshevik regime the century-old importance of formal educational credentials became a far more explicit demand for specialized technical training and, of course, officialdom itself has continued to operate and grow.

That there was some discontinuity following the Revolution of 1917 is hardly surprising, but the early nineteenth century does not have a comparable landmark. It is nevertheless clear that in the course of a generation civil officialdom underwent substantial change. Peter I had certainly emphasized training of the nobility, but not training directed at preparing civil officials in institutions designed for that purpose. Throughout the eighteenth century it was assumed that prior military experience, frequently including education in the Cadet Corps, was adequate preparation for the upper ranks of civil officialdom. For lower-level clerkships, apprenticeship in an office from a tender age was the normal pattern. Beginning in the early nineteenth century, however, qualifications came to be set in terms of reaching specified levels of formal education ...

The second strand that seems to end in the late eighteenth and early nineteenth century is the great importance of family ties ... The combination of growth in size and, in the early nineteenth century, increased emphasis on formal education inevitably produced a more impersonal institution, although family ties, friendship and patronage undoubtedly continued to play a role in appointments and promotions.

The third major thread that ends in the late eighteenth – early nineteenth century is the unity of military and civilian service at the upper level. From the seventeenth century, and possibly even earlier, the lower-level positions in central service were largely filled with life-time employees and a few of them rose to important posts, but the normal career patterns of high officials in the seventeenth and eighteenth centuries was one that included both civil and military assignments, frequently so intermingled as to preclude designating the official as primarily one or the other. From the early nineteenth century forward to the present day, although ex-military men are still to be found, the characteristic career pattern at all levels increasingly came to be one of purely civil service. (Pintner and Rowney, 1980, pp.373–5).

That is to say, in some respects the Tsarist civil service was becoming a 'bureaucracy' in the Weberian sense during the nineteenth century. That it appears to have done so in the context of an absolutist monarchy (whose last incumbent, Nicholas II, was still asserting the Divine Right of Kings at the beginning of the twentieth century) is significant: for it suggests that there were general trends at work changing the nature of the European state during the nineteenth century perhaps independently of formal constitutional arrangements. What might these have been?

Here is where your reading of Anderson, and particularly of his Chapter 2 ('The mechanics of government') comes in. If you have not already read this chapter carefully, do it now.

Exercise   As you no doubt have noted from this reading, Anderson does not conveniently offer a separate section on bureaucracy and state structures, although he does present some relevant information at various points in Chapter 2. Especially worth considering are the implications of Anderson's comments on p.102: that 'the statesmen of the 1850s and 1860s, sometimes against their will, were being carried by events into an age dominated by size and quantity and by the rationality or pseudo-rationality which these generate'; and that the 'regimes of the 1850s and 1860s were therefore in many cases progressive, administratively if not politically'. Why was this happening? And how might you explain why, whereas Pintner and Rowney identify the early nineteenth and early twentieth centuries as crucial periods of change for Russian officialdom, Anderson identifies the mid-nineteenth century.

Discussion   Among the reasons, touched on by Anderson (pp.101–2), why the changes he outlined were occurring are:

1   the need to generate increasing amounts of accurate information (census statistics, information necessary for levying taxes, etc.);

2   the growth of concern to inspect (e.g. factories, housing, bridges) and control (those in receipt of some form of social provision);

3   the expansion of the numbers of people employed by the state (as teachers, medical officers, employees of state-owned railways);

4   the perceived need for a professionally trained corps of civil servants to administer an increasingly complex economy and society.

As Anderson notes, the increasing number and complexity of the tasks which the state's servants were expected to carry out, 'the multiplication in every advanced state ... of new agencies of social provision and control was rapidly increasing the element of professional expertise in the ordering of society' (p.102) – that is, of bureaucracy. In other words, urbanization, industrialization, and population growth gave rise to a need for more extensive and centralized social organization of the sort which a state bureaucracy provides.

The difference between the perspectives offered by Pintner and Rowney on the one hand and by Anderson on the other stem primarily from the fact that they are concerned with rather different things: the issue addressed in the quotation by Pintner and Rowney is *how* officials are recruited, trained and operate, which altered at the beginning of the nineteenth century; the issue addressed by Anderson concerns *what* tasks they carry out, and he sees these developing in mid-century in response to the problems posed by an increasingly urban-industrial society. (The peculiarities of Russia's development are probably of less relevance here; the early nineteenth century saw crucial changes in how French and German officials were recruited as well, as we have seen.)

The short outline by Pintner and Rowney offered above, of changes in Tsarist Russia during the nineteenth century, highlights another important development: that the civil service became more distinctly 'civil', as opposed to military. One of the main reasons for this development is that the state's tasks expanded far beyond things associated to a greater or lesser extent with the military (foreign affairs, fighting wars), so that expertise in explicitly non-military matters was required by an increasing number of the state's servants. The increasing number and complexity of the tasks it faced, and the increasing size of the establishment required to meet these tasks, meant that service in state administrations became more a profession whose members required expertise in these tasks.

A similar parallel development may be seen *within* the military, which increasingly came to require technical expertise which in turn required specific training and for which noble birth did not suffice. As Norman Stone has noted, in the introduction to his study of the Russian Army during the First World War:

> As the European arms-race went ahead, armies became much larger, and the pace of technological change increased. Training had to go beyond the academic drilling of the past, for the men to be given essential skills, as their weapons grew more complex. The composition of the officers' corps had to change: courage had to make way for trigonometry, the horse for the internal combustion engine. Modernization altered the terms of military relationships: it altered the roles of cavalry, artillery, fortresses, infantry, and sometimes abolished their role. To make the necessary changes, and to plan for war in accordance with them, armies needed a central planning body, the dictates of which might over-ride the vested interest of the past. (Stone, 1975, p.19)

Thus the pace of technological change and the increasing size of the armed forces in the nineteenth century – and even more so in the twentieth – has tended to turn armies more into the sorts of bureaucratic organizations described above.

However, when considering the Russian bureaucracy during the nineteenth century, we need also to note the ways in which its development diverged significantly from the Weberian model. It did so in two important and interrelated respects. The first is that – unlike the case in France or Prussia/Germany – Tsarist Russia never really was a *Rechtsstaat*, a state grounded in law, in which practices such as arbitrary arrest are not accepted and where there is a requirement to observe procedural proprieties. Bureaucratic practice in Tsarist Russia was not subordinate to the rule of law, but instead remained (despite the efforts of Tsar Alexander II to create a *Rechtsstaat*) quite arbitrary. The extreme centralization of the Russian state and the mass of unjust and unwieldy laws which officials were expected to apply virtually guaranteed arbitrary behaviour. According to Pintner and Rowney (1980, p.283), what was emerging in nineteenth-century Russia was 'not a *Rechtsstaat*, a law-state, but a bureaucratic state in which bureaucratic principles of procedure ... gradually displace the significance and the need for law'. This was related to the second important respect in which Russian bureaucratic practice differed from Weberian ideal-typical behaviour: the Tsarist bureaucracy was quite spectacularly corrupt, so that it bore similarities to the 'venal' office-holding of the *ancien regime*. It is to this aspect of bureaucratic practice which we now turn.

Bureaucracy and corruption

Richard Pipes, who notes the 'notorious venality of Russian officials, especially those working in the provinces, and most of all in provinces far removed from the capital cities', ascribed this to the way in which the state remunerated its servants: 'It was inherent in a government which, lacking funds to pay for the administration, not only had for centuries paid its civil servants no salary, but had insisted that they feed themselves from official business' (Pipes, 1977, p.282). Although some nineteenth-century Russian officials were conscientious, intelligent and worked hard to modernize their backward country, the Russian bureaucracy earned its reputation for laziness and corruption. Stories of corruption abounded: of leading officials in St Petersburg stealing huge sums from the public purse; of medium-ranking bureaucrats who terrorized and extorted tribute from the local population; of officials who took full advantage of opportunities to put friends and relatives onto the state payroll (H. Seton-Watson, 1967, pp.208–12). This was a far cry from a bureaucracy in which (as Weber saw it) officials were 'remunerated by fixed salaries in money, for the most part with a right to pensions' and the civil servant was 'subject to strict and systematic discipline and control in the conduct of his office'.

The question which arises from this is whether the Russian bureaucracy, in so deviating from the Weberian model, was perhaps fairly typical of European state bureaucracies in the nineteenth century (and not only in the nineteenth century). Perhaps extensive corruption and the absence of the effective rule of law may have been more the rule than the exception, and perhaps practices changed rather less since the eighteenth century than we might imagine. Concluding a discussion of the problems associated with the Tsarist bureaucracy in the middle of the nineteenth century, Hugh Seton-Watson noted:

> It may indeed be argued that in a poor and backward country, with very few educated persons, corruption is needed to make the wheels of the state machine turn, and that nepotism is a necessary substitute for the welfare state. This problem is not limited in space to Russia, or in time to the mid-nineteenth century. (H. Seton-Watson, 1967, p.212)

When thinking about how Europe was governed and administered during the nineteenth century, we need to keep in mind that most of the continent was 'poor and backward'. (Students of urban government in the United States during the late nineteenth century could remind us that such corruption was rife there as well, and formed a 'substitute for the welfare state' not only in 'poor and backward' countries.) Perhaps the high standards which came to be expected for German and British civil servants during the nineteenth century, while they more closely matched to the model offered by Weber, were the exception rather than the rule.

However, as we have noted above, Weber described the way things ideally ought to work, not how they actually worked in practice. Even in the two classic bureaucratic states, France and Prussia, in practice the civil service never really met the ideal of neutrality above particular interests. In the France of Napoleon III, notes Roger Magraw, 'teachers and postal officials were expected to act as political agents for the regime'

(Magraw, 1983, p.167). In Prussia, whose bureaucracy had gained a repu-tation of incorruptibility and had provided the model for Weber's typol-ogy, the activities of the state's servants also diverged from the ideal. The Prussian disciplinary law of 1852, for example, enlarged the category of 'political' civil servants, who consequently were subject to dismissal for failure to toe the political line. In the elections of 1882 Prussian civil ser-vants were reminded of their 'duty' to support government policy (Caplan, 1979, p.306) and, as Peter-Christian Witt has shown in his revealing examination of the corruption and inefficiency of Prussian bureaucrats, Prussian *Landräte* before the First World War often allowed local lan-downers to escape their tax liabilities while taking care to ensure that the taxes of lesser citizens were assessed in full (Witt, 1974).

Perhaps the major change in the nineteenth century was not that bureaucracy actually became less corrupt (something which would be difficult to measure even if it were so), but that increasingly it was felt that government bureaucrats should not be corrupt – that they had a certain responsibility for which they were paid a salary and that private interest should not determine their public behaviour. It was this which Weber described as an ideal type, when he defined a bureaucracy in terms of its remuneration and its being 'subject to strict and systematic discipline'. The suggestion here is that the key shift may have been in terms less of actual behaviour than of expectations: that it became illegitimate to expect private payment for the performance of a public function, even if many officials in fact did so.

Life under bureaucratic rule

Now we need to look outwards from state bureaucracies, beyond what they were and how they developed to what they did and what effects their activi-ties had on the rest of European humanity. How did the growing bureaucratization of government shape the lives of Europeans in the nineteenth century? Two descriptions (both by American observers) of life in Europe before the First World War – the first in Russia, the second in Germany – give some flavour of how bureaucratic regulations affected peo-ple in their everyday lives. The first comes from George Kennan (the great uncle of the George Kennan who was chargé at the American Embassy in Moscow during the Second World War and subsequently became the architect of the United States' policy of 'containment' vis-à-vis the Soviet Union), writing in 1888–9:

> If you are a Russian, and wish to establish a newspaper, you must ask the permission of the Minister of the Interior. If you wish to open a Sunday-school, or any other sort of school, whether in a neglected slum of St Petersburg or in a native village in Kamchatka, you must ask the permission of the Minister of Public Instruction. If you wish to give a concert or to get up tableaux for the benefit of an orphan asy-lum, you must ask permission of the nearest representative of the Minister of the Interior, then submit your programme of exercises to a censor for approval or revision, and finally hand over the proceeds of

the entertainment to the police, to be embezzled or given to the orphan asylum, as it may happen. If you wish to sell newspapers on the street, you must get permission, be registered in the books of the police, and wear a numbered brass plate as big as a saucer around your neck. If you wish to open a drug-store, a printing office, a photograph-gallery, or a book-store, you must get permission. If you are a photographer and desire to change the location of your place of business, you must get permission. If you are a student and go to a public library to consult Lyell's *Principles of Geology* or Spencer's *Social Statistics*, you will find that you cannot even look at such dangerous and incendiary volumes without special permission. If you are a physician, you must get permission before you can practice, and then, if you do not wish to respond to calls in the night, you must have permission to refuse to go; furthermore, if you wish to prescribe what are known in Russia as 'powerfully acting' medicines, you must have special permission, or the druggist will not dare to fill your prescriptions. If you are a peasant and wish to build a bath-house on your premises, you must get permission. If you wish to thresh out your grain in the evening by candle-light, you must get permission or bribe the police. If you wish to go more than fifteen miles away from your home, you must get permission. If you are a foreign traveler, you must get permission to come into the Empire, permission to go out of it, permission to stay longer than six months, and must notify the police every time you change your boarding-place. In short, you cannot live, move, or have your being in the Russian Empire without permission. (George Kennan, 'The Russian Police', *The Century Illustrated Magazine*, vol. xxxvii (1888–9), pp.890–2; quoted in Pipes, 1977, p.308)

The second, about Imperial Germany, was written in 1914 by the American observer of European police forces Raymond Fosdick:

On every side and at every turn, the German citizen is confronted by newly adopted police regulations. Thus in Berlin, the Police President has recently issued ordinances regulating the color of automobiles, the length of hatpins and the methods of purchasing fish and fowl ... In Stuttgart, a driver may not snap his whip as he guides his horses in the street; a customer may not fall asleep in a restaurant or a weary man on a park bench; a barber may not keep his official trade card in an inconspicuous place; a cab-driver may not leave his position in front of the railway station during the hours in which the police decree he shall be on duty; a driver may not hold his reins improperly or go through the public streets without having the owner's name in a conspicuous place on his cart or carriage; a delivery boy may not coast on a hand-cart or carriage; a passenger may not alight from a train on the side away from the platform or while the train is in motion; children may not slide on a slippery sidewalk; a citizen may not be impertinent to a public official on duty nor offer any affront to his dignity. These regulations are not only negative, they are often positive; not only general, but particular and directed against specific parties. Thus a house owner *must* sprinkle his street in hot weather when ordered by the police or a certain striker *must* refrain from picketing when so directed or a given contractor *must* remove building encumbrances on demand. (Raymond B. Fosdick, *European Police Systems*, 1915, pp. 27–8; quoted in Evans, 1982, p.6)

Exercise   Think about the two quotes you have just read and make a note of any similarities and differences between them.

Discussion   The similarities between these two passages are remarkable. However, it is worth noting that both have been used to establish the uniqueness of the Russian and German empires respectively. Richard Pipes, in his *Russia under the Old Regime*, quotes Kennan to help demonstrate how in Russia, 'unlike the rest of Europe to which Russia belongs by virtue of her location, race and religion – society has proven unable to impose on political authority any kind of effective restraints', and that the country yielded 'to a police regime which in effect has been in power there ever since' (Pipes, 1977, p.xvii). Similarly, the Fosdick quotation periodically is hauled out to demonstrate that Germans were regimented to an extraordinary extent. Both countries' historiographies are (in this context perhaps paradoxically) characterized by important interpretations which stress their uniqueness, and the place of their states and state bureaucracies plays an important role here.

It also is worth observing that both passages are by Americans; accordingly, the comments may well reflect as much, if not more, the Anglo-Saxon perspectives of their authors (i.e. the perspectives of observers accustomed to life in a developed country in which the state played a remarkably limited role during the nineteenth century and where police controls and legal regulation was minimal) than actual conditions in Imperial Germany and Imperial Russia.

Certainly both the passages suggest that state bureaucrats – and especially the police – kept constant and comprehensive control over populations whose lives were increasingly regulated by the state and its laws by the end of the nineteenth century. Yet one might question how much they actually tell us about the extent to which the state's bureaucracies came to intervene in the lives of its subjects. How much of what is described is really about the new powers of a bureaucracy? Before the advent of modern state bureaucracies, and before peasant emancipation, would not many similar forms of control have been exercised by the lord over his immediate subjects? Were not prohibitions and controls over certain forms of behaviour, as described by Kennan and Fosdick, quite compatible with the old *Polizey-Staat* which really precedes the modern bureaucratic state? The answer to these questions probably should take the form of a qualified yes – that state control over its subjects was not new in the nineteenth century, although many aspects of that control, especially insofar as it involved the regulation of an increasingly industrialized society, were. Indeed, they outline only a fraction of the points of intersection between state bureaucracies and people in the nineteenth century, in which 'government and subject or citizen were inevitably linked by daily bonds, as never before' (Hobsbawm, 1992, p.81).

Although we can trace the bureaucratic state with which we are familiar to developments in nineteenth-century Europe, we need to remember that even during the late nineteenth century the European continent was hardly crawling with government bureaucrats. Compared with most

European societies in the twentieth century, nineteenth-century Europe was still relatively lightly administered and bureaucrats were, by today's standards, thin on the ground. To give one revealing example: in 1826 the regional administrative office of the Prussian administrative region of Marienwerder (which covered 318 square miles and contained roughly 330,000 inhabitants) had only 59 employees, most of them messengers, clerks and junior officials (Sheehan, 1989, p.439). Even the large figures given earlier for civil servants in France and Prussia as a whole (as well as the much larger figures for the German Reich after 1871, which include hundreds of thousands of postal and railway employees) still appear relatively modest when set against the huge state bureaucracies which have grown up in twentieth-century Europe.

Perhaps the most striking illustration of the relative scarcity of bureaucrats is the Russian Empire, where 'you cannot live, move, or have your being ... without permission'. There, as Richard Pipes points out (notwithstanding his concern to trace the origins of the Russian bureaucratic police state), in the middle of the century there were only about 11 to 13 civil servants per 10,000 inhabitants in the Russian Empire – a ratio 'three to four times below that prevailing at the same time in western Europe' – and were 'certainly administratively understaffed' (Pipes, 1977, p.281). This fact underlay the inefficiency, arbitrariness and corruption of the Russian bureaucracy, and suggests that hopes and fears of bureaucratic control in nineteenth-century Europe fell far short of the reality.

We need to consider, therefore, what effect state bureaucracies, and the mass of regulations they issued and enforced, in fact had on the great mass of people across the European continent. (Here it is worth noting that, in the passages reproduced above, Kennan and Fosdick were describing life essentially in cities: Fosdick was writing about Berlin, not some farming village in eastern Prussia; and many of Kennan's examples make sense only in urban settings – in a country which was predominantly rural.) The question is particularly important when looking at largely peasant societies – and, despite industrialization in many regions, nineteenth-century Europe still was composed mainly of peasant societies. A distinction such as that often made in post-unification Italy, between 'legal' Italy (of king, parliament, politicians and bureaucrats, concentrated in the capital) and 'real' Italy (of poor, often illiterate rural society), could have been applied to much of nineteenth-century Europe. In Italy, and not only in the south but also in the economically more advanced north as well, 'a great gulf separated the social classes in the countryside, isolating the peasantry from the main stream of national life and leaving it outside the state to which it did not seem to belong' (C. Seton-Watson, 1967, p.25.) These were the parts of society that bureaucracy did not reach.

Such observations need not have been limited to Italy. Most European societies were peasant societies in the nineteenth century, and in much of Europe a great gulf separated the social classes in the countryside, isolating the peasantry from the main stream of national life and leaving it outside the state to which it did not seem to belong – and largely outside the reach of government administration and government bureaucrats in terms of day-to-day activities. Of course, this was changing. By the final decades of the nineteenth century the growth of industrial economies (which were increasingly regulated, by the state and its inspectors), the development of state welfare institutions and the beginnings social insurance legislation were bringing a growing number of Europeans (still largely in northern and western Europe) into regular contact with state bureaucracies. This, however, is a story which forms the subject of Unit 5, on welfare, where you will learn more about how state bureaucracies affected people's everyday lives.

Bureaucracy and modernity?

Finally, to close this unit, you are offered a rather different perspective on European bureaucracies. In much of what you have read thus far the stress has been upon the role of bureaucracy and the state in nineteenth-century Europe in shaping the modern world which we inhabit. Our view of the nineteenth century has been essentially forward looking. For a final exercise, we include an important perspective from which the history of Europe (and its bureaucracies) in the nineteenth century is seen in precisely the other way, as backward looking: from Arno Mayer's polemical text, published in 1981, *The Persistence of the Old Regime. Europe to the Great War.* Mayer set out to question the view that the nineteenth century saw the end of the *ancien regime* in Europe and the advent of our modern world – a view which, I must admit, underpins my writing of this unit. Introducing his book, Mayer wrote:

> This book does not offer a balanced interpretation of Europe between 1848 and 1914. To counteract the chronic overstatement of the unfolding and ultimate triumph of modernity ... it will concentrate on the persistence of the old order. The conventional wisdom is still that Europe broke out of its *ancien regime* and approached or crossed the threshold of modernity well before 1914 ... It is the thesis of this book that the 'premodern' elements were not the decaying and fragile remnants of an all but vanished past but the very essence of Europe's incumbent civil and political societies. (Mayer, 1981, pp.5–6)

Among the subjects to which Mayer looked in order to buttress his thesis was the composition of European bureaucracies. It is to this which we now turn.

Exercise   Please now read Offprint 2. How does Mayer's argument relate to the subject of this unit?

Discussion   In this extract, Mayer challenges some of the assumptions underlying what you have read here thus far. Note, for example, the rhetorical questions he poses at the outset, including: 'Did service in the state ministries make them (i.e. the officials) into agents of bureaucratic rationalism and professionalism, as defined by Max Weber?' Mayer obviously has his doubts. He points to the continued strong representation of the nobility in the upper reaches of the bureaucracies of European states in the nineteenth century, and points to the continued narrowness of the social base of recruitment and promotion within civil-service establishments. He concludes that 'down to 1914 the "steel frame" of Europe's political societies continued to be heavily feudal and nobilitarian'. In this, he is probably right. But does this mean that Weber was wrong, or that nineteenth-century European state bureaucracies were not a force for modernization – perhaps despite the origins or political preferences of the bureaucrats themselves? That will be for you to judge.

References

Caplan, J. (1979), ' "The imaginary universality of particular interests": The "tradition" of the civil service in German history', *Social History*, vol. iv, no. 2.

Church, C. (1981), *Revolution and Red Tape. The French Ministerial Bureaucracy 1770–1850*, Clarendon Press, Oxford.

Evans, R. J. (1982), 'Introduction: the sociological interpretation of German labour history', in R. J. Evans (ed.), *The German Working Class 1888–1933*, Croom Helm, London.

Geyer, M. (1984), 'The state in National Socialist Germany', in C. Bright and S. Harding (eds), *Statemaking and Social Movements. Essays in History and Theory*, The University of Michigan Press, Ann Arbor.

Hintze, O. (1981), 'Der Beamtenstand', in O. Hintze, *Beamtentum und Bürokratie*, Vandenhoeck & Ruprecht, Göttingen.

Hobsbawm, E.J. (1992), *Nations and Nationalism since 1870. Programme, Myth, Reality*, 2nd. edn, Cambridge University Press, Cambridge.

Koselleck, R. (1989), *Preußen zwischen Reform und Revolution. Allgemeines Landrecht, Verwaltung und soziale Bewegung von 1791 bis 1848*, Deutscher Taschenbuch Verlag, Munich.

Magraw, R. (1983), *France 1815–1914. The Bourgeois Century*, Fontana, London.

Mann, M. (1993), *The Sources of Social Power. Volume II. The Rise of Classes and Nation-States, 1760–1914*, Cambridge University Press, Cambridge.

Mayer, A. J. (1981), *The Persistence of the Old Regime. Europe to the Great War*, Croom Helm, London.

Mommsen, W. J.(1974), *The Age of Bureaucracy. Perspectives on the Political Sociology of Max Weber*, Basil Blackwell, Oxford.

Pintner, W. M. and Rowney, D. K. (1980), 'Officialdom and Bureaucratization: Conclusion', in W. M. Pintner and D. K. Rowney (eds), *Russian Officialdom: The Bureaucratization of Russian Society from the Seventeenth to the Twentieth Century*, Macmillan, London and Basingstoke.

Pipes, R. (1977), *Russia under the Old Regime*, Penguin Books, Harmondsworth.

Rosenberg, H. (1966), *Bureaucracy, Aristocracy and Autocracy. The Prussian Experience 1660–1815*, Beacon Press, Boston.

Seton-Watson, C. (1967), *Italy from Liberalism to Fascism, 1870–1925*, Methuen, London.

Seton-Watson, H. (1967), *The Russian Empire 1801–1917*, Oxford University Press, Oxford.

Sheehan, J. J.(1989), *German History 1770–1866*, Oxford University Press, Oxford.

Stone, N. (1975), *The Eastern Front 1914–1917*, Hodder and Stoughton, London.

Weber, M. (1978), *Economy and Society. An Outline of Interpretive Sociology*, edited by Guenther Roth and Claus Wittich, The University of California Press, Berkeley, Los Angeles and London.

Witt, P-C. (1974), 'Der preussische Landrat als Steuerbeamte 1891–1918. Bemerkungen zur politischen und sozialen Funktion des deutschen Beamtentums', in I. Geiss and B-J. Wendt (eds), *Deutschland in der Weltpolitik des 19. und 20. Jahrhunderts*, Droste Verlag, Düsseldorf.

Wunder, B. (1986), *Geschichte der Bürokratie in Deutschland*, Suhrkamp Verlag, Frankfurt/Main.

Zeldin, T.(1973), *France 1848–1945. Volume I. Ambition, Love, Politics*, Oxford University Press, Oxford.

Unit 4
Legitimate force

Prepared for the course team by
Clive Emsley

Contents

Study timetable

Weeks of Study	Texts	Video	AC
2	Unit 4; Documents I.15–I.24; Anderson		

Aims

The aims of this unit are to encourage you to think about:

1   what constituted the legitimate force within the nineteenth-century state;

2   the role of this force in defending the state;

3   the differences between different states;

4   the acceptance of this force by the people living in the different states.

Introduction

For centuries in Europe monarchs and governments had sought to limit the ability of private individuals to employ force on their own behalf. By the beginning of the nineteenth century most governments had succeeded in acquiring a monopoly of force within their frontiers; they declared this to be the only legitimate force in the country, and they employed it against both internal and external enemies.

The military

Exercise The obvious, principal role of an army is to fight a country's international wars. I want you to read Anderson chapter 6, and to note down the following.

1   What other main role fell to European armies, particularly in the first half of the nineteenth century, and what subsidiary roles the armies might be said to have played (for the latter look particularly carefully at pp.311–13 and 315)?

2   In what way the armies might be said to reflect the social structure of the states which they served, what changes occurred in the armies during the period, and what concerns these generated, especially in Germany?

Specimen Answers 1   Anderson notes (p.293) that in the period 1815–48 armies were frequently used to maintain internal order and the status quo. While I expect you to have remembered, it is worth noting that, earlier in the book when discussing the Revolutions of 1848 (p.98), he writes: 'Throughout central and eastern Europe, perhaps even in France, the ultimate guarantee of political stability was now an army of peasant conscripts, poorly-educated and unsympathetic to town-bred radicals, officered by landowners or at least members of well-to-do families'. Anderson suggests (pp.311–12) that in France and Prussia after 1871, the armies became national symbols: in the former the army was particularly a focus for national unity and regeneration following military defeat; in the latter the army's success gave it enormous prestige and allowed its senior officers to acquire independence of, and precedence over, civilian authority. He notes also the opportunities which the military gave for educating and indoctrinating young men conscripted into the ranks of different armies; here he singles out Russia (p.313) and Germany (p.315).

2   The armies were not precise replica of the social structure, nevertheless they did reflect its extremes. The bulk of the conscripts were drawn from the poorest in society, generally from the peasantry and from those who could not afford to provide a substitute. The officers were becoming more and more professional, but aristocratic influence

remained strong especially in guards and cavalry regiments, and at the top (pp.294–6). In Germany towards the end of the century there was concern that the dilution of the officer corps, together with making the army truly national and representative, by taking more conscripts for a shorter time, would potentially weaken its loyalty to the regime (p.315).

During the eighteenth century some Enlightenment thinkers had extolled the idea of a citizen army, a nationalist militia of free men, as opposed to the strictly regimented, standing armies of absolutist monarchs. The American Revolution provided an example of such a militia; the French Revolution provided another. The decree of the *levée en masse* in August 1793 equated citizenship with military obligation. It declared:

> The young men shall go to battle; the married men shall make arms and transport provisions; the women shall make tents and uniforms, and shall serve in the hospitals; the children shall make old clothes into bandages; the old men shall go out into the public squares to boost the soldier's courage and to preach the unity of the republic and the hatred of kings. (*Le Moniteur*, 25 Aug. 1793; my translation)

Napoleon continued the practice of mass conscription; many of his enemies had to introduce similar systems to defeat him, notably Prussia who, in 1813–14 put more men into the field proportionate to her population than any other power. But, of course, neither Napoleon nor the Prussian reformers were keen to equate military obligation and democratic citizenship. The intention was rather to oblige men to serve in the armed forces, and, through military discipline, to mould them while they served. However, the idea of the citizen army continued to be a potent one.

Most of the European armies of the nineteenth century had auxiliaries and reserves. The latter were usually men who had served in the regular army. In the first half of the century the Prussian army appeared large on paper because of its reserve system. Those conscripts who were called up at the age of twenty and could not arrange a substitute, served with the colours for three years. Back in civilian life they then spent two years in the reserve, and finally moved, until they were 40, to the *Landwehr*, which was organized on a regional basis, and officered by the local gentry. As well as men who had served in the regular army, the *Landwehr* also included those who had not been called up, but the system did not work well in emergencies. In 1831, for example, Prussia felt threatened as her rulers nervously watched peasant insurrection just beyond her eastern frontiers, and revolution in Belgium and France. The only way to meet any threat was to call out the *Landwehr*. The regular army considered this humiliating having little time for the *Landwehr's* civilian, regional organization. Members of the *Landwehr* themselves were greatly vexed at being torn from their civilian lives. The 1848 Revolution made the Prussian military even more suspicious of the organization and reliability of the *Landwehr*, and the reforms of General von Roon (see Unit 1) in the early 1860s tied the system much closer to the regular army by abolishing the local control and introducing regular army officers.

France, for the first half of the century, possessed a National Guard which maintained some of the elements of the citizen army. The National Guard had been created as a militia to preserve internal order during the French Revolution. It had been incorporated into the line army, but was revived under Napoleon and saw some action, principally when the allies invaded France in 1814. Charles X abolished the Guard in 1827. He considered it politically too liberal and hence a threat to his regime. But though abolishing it, Charles failed to call in the men's weapons, and the Parisian guardsmen duly demonstrated their liberalism in the July Revolution in 1830 by siding with the insurrection in large numbers. Louis Philippe revived the Guard, again specifically to preserve internal order; membership was to depend on property. The respectable National Guardsmen of Lyon played a prominent role in the suppression of the insurrections by the city's silk weavers in 1831 and 1834. In the Revolution of 1848 membership was thrown open to all, and in the savage fighting of the June Days in Paris National Guardsmen fought on both sides of the barricades. Napoleon III abolished the force when he came to power, but he revived it again at the end of the 1860s along the lines of the Prussian *Landwehr* in the hope that it would provide him with a significant reserve. National Guardsmen were among the troops who made the heroic defence of Paris against the Germans during the siege of September 1870 to January 1871. The reluctance of some of the National Guard units to give up their weapons was the spark which led to the insurrection of the Paris Commune.

Britain had no conscription, but it did have a variety of auxiliary forces in the nineteenth century. During the Napoleonic wars much home defence was left in the hands of militia and volunteers. Every county had a militia regiment recruited by a ballot of men aged between 18 and 45, and in wartime the militia was embodied on a regular footing; it could not, however, be deployed outside the country. The volunteers were genuine citizen soldiers who turned out once a week to train in case the French invaded; they were also called out when internal disorder required a military presence and no regulars or militia were available. Tens of thousands of volunteers came forward during the wars; many served for purely patriotic motives, but without doubt others did so because the early acts of parliament authorizing volunteer corps exempted their members from the militia ballot. At the end of the Napoleonic wars the militia was stood down and allowed to decay; for the most part, the volunteers were also disbanded, but the elegant yeomanry cavalry, generally recruited from the relatively well-off, remained – primarily for internal police duties. Both militia and volunteers were subsequently revived, particularly when the Second Empire was established in France and there was concern in Britain that Napoleon III had plans for crossing the Channel similar to those of his uncle half a century before.

Exercise   1   Can you perceive of any problems in using auxiliary forces for internal order?

2   Can you perceive of any problems in relying too heavily on auxiliary forces instead of regular troops for fighting wars?

Specimen Answers   1   There was the possibility that auxiliaries would not be prepared to act in cases of internal disorder. It could be, after all, that they were being required to act against friends and neighbours.

2   There are two points here. First, the increasing sophistication of weaponry meant that men required training in its use. The size of armies, the way that they were moved in vast numbers by railways, required discipline and organization, again the product of training. Second, there was the possibility that armed citizens, unhappy with their government, might seek to use their weaponry against that government; while I do not expect you to know this, the performance of Parisian National Guards on a succession of occasions offers an example. There were also times during the Napoleonic wars when the British government grew concerned about some of the attitudes expressed by Volunteers.

In Britain during and immediately after the Napoleonic wars the use of Yeomanry units to suppress popular disorder appears, on occasions, to have aggravated the situation. The best example was the 'Peterloo' massacre in 1819, when the Manchester Yeomanry Cavalry, recruited from the sons of mill owners and gentry, was ordered against a radical, plebeian crowd. The Yeomen bungled their advance and class antagonism flared between them and the crowd. In the end the Yeomanry had to be rescued by regular cavalry. A quarter of a century later the central government was advising against the use of the gentlemen of the yeomanry cavalry to suppress any Chartist disorder in case their appearance inflamed a situation.

It remained possible, though it was very rare, for enthusiastic volunteers inspired by an ideal, to overcome regular troops. The best examples of such are the men who fought with Garibaldi during the Italian wars of independence. Garibaldi was a better guerrilla leader than field commander yet, in 1849, he inspired a heroic defence of the Roman Republic with a motley army. In 1860 he led a mixed bag of volunteers, the famous '1000', to Sicily. At Calatafini, on 15 May these volunteers, few of whom had any military training, armed for the most part with out-of-date muskets, defeated a Neopolitan army twice their size by an enthusiastic, but potentially suicidal, charge up a hill in the heat of the afternoon. Seven years later another enthusiastic assault by *Garibaldini* at Mentana, this time against a French army armed with the new *chassepot* rifle, met with an altogether different, and rather more predictable result. In Britain the battle of Mentana was one of the examples commonly used by the military press to warn against further development of the volunteer forces. In France the heroic, historical image of the men raised by the *levée en masse* during the Revolution kept the idea of the citizen army popular, especially among the political left; Communards appealed to this image, and in 1911 the socialist leader Jean Jaurès published *L'armée nouvelle* (the new army) arguing for a citizen army and reflecting his party's concerns about professional soldiers and élitist academies for military officers.

Police and gendarmerie

Exercise Read Anderson pp.159–62 and look also at the Metternich quote on p.3, then answer the following questions.

1 What is the general picture which Anderson gives of police development during the nineteenth century?

2 What reasons does Anderson give for the development of the police?

3 Is Metternich talking about the same kind of police as Anderson, if not, what sort of policing does he have in mind in this quotation?

Specimen Answers 1 Anderson suggests that police forces in the first half of the century were small and inadequate, but that in the second half of the century they became larger and more efficient.

2 He stresses the growth of cities, with ensuing problems of crime and disorder, as being central to police development, together with the fact that governments believed that they needed something other than military force to deal with such problems.

3 Metternich did not see himself as supervising the uniformed men who patrolled city streets, rather he is referring to what we would probably call political policing.

Police and policing, as can be seen from these few pages in Anderson, can cover a variety of tasks and also a variety of organizations. Anderson specifically mentions urban police and rural gendarmes. While there is a popular English assumption that all French police are gendarmes (indeed a French thesis presented at the end of the 1970s suggested that some people in France were equally mistaken (Dootjes-Dussuyer, 1979, p.64)) this is, in fact, quite wrong. Urban or municipal police during the nineteenth century were generally civilian.

In capital cities across Europe they were usually directly responsible to the central government; in other towns and cities there could be some national direction and supervision, but equally often the men were responsible to local government. Gendarmes, generally speaking, were soldiers. They were armed and equipped like soldiers and came under the responsibility of the ministry of war. And they were not just a French phenomenon; most of the German states had gendarmeries (sometimes called *Landjägers*) as did Belgium; the Dutch *Koninklijke Marechaussee*, the Italian *Carabinieri* and the Spanish *Guardia Civil*, were similar, as were the Royal Irish Constabulary and the Russia Gendarmerie, though the latter two did not come under a war ministry. Political police too came in a variety of forms; in Russia for most of the century the Third Section of the Imperial Chancellory, which was responsible for political policing, also controlled the Gendarmerie. The term 'political police' was usually covered by a euphemism; but such organizations were, naturally, responsible to central government.

Capital city police, municipal police, gendarmeries all developed as bureaucratic, hierarchical institutions during the nineteenth century – another example of the burgeoning state bureaucracies. The word 'police' – *police*, *Polizei*, *polizia* – began to be used commonly throughout Europe to describe at least the civilian forces. Before the nineteenth century it had a rather different meaning.

Police comes from the Greek word *politeia*, referring to all things affecting the survival and well-being of the *polis* (the city state). During the seventeenth and eighteenth centuries the word was used in Europe as a synonym for government. In France, increasingly it referred to the government of a city. In the German lands it was often tied with the ideal results of government. According to one of the key thinkers of the German Enlightenment, Johann Heinrich Gottlieb von Justi:

> Police, in the broad understanding of the term, refers to all those measures in the internal affairs of a nation through which the wealth of the state may be more permanently established and multiplied, the forces of the state better used and, in general, the happiness of the commonality promoted ...
>
> Police, in a narrow sense of the term, refers to all that which is required for the proper condition of civil life, and in particular for the maintenance of good order and discipline amongst subjects, and those measures which promote the flourishing and growth of trade ... (quoted in Lüdtke, 1989, p.205)

Enlightened despots working towards this end were happy to have their regimes described individually as a 'police state' (*Polizeistaat*). *Polizei* ('Police') covered both the *Sicherheit* (security) and the *Wohlfahrt* (welfare) of the prince's subjects. Historians studying these states have also used the term 'welfare state' (*Wohlfahrtstaat*) to describe best what the princes considered they were seeking to establish and preserve for their people.

As with much else in the late seventeenth and eighteenth centuries, enlightened despots looked to France for their police models. The French were considered to have the most efficient police forces in Europe. In Paris there was an organization responsible for everything from crime prevention patrols to wet nurses and from markets to street lighting, directed by the *lieutenant général de police de Paris* – a post created by Louis XIV in 1667. In the countryside the roads were patrolled by mounted troopers of the *maréchaussée* – the men of the marshals of France, originally established to keep the king's armies in check, but who had acquired considerable civilian jurisdiction particularly towards the end of the seventeenth century. The *maréchaussée* was never more than 3800 men, but it was generally perceived as competent and effective. At the beginning of the French Revolution the *maréchaussée* was doubled in size and given a new name, *la Gendarmerie Nationale*. In 1791 every town with a population of 5000 or more was required to have a *commissaire* of police whose appointment was, under Napoleon and subsequently, to be approved by the central government; the decision on how many policemen (*sergents de ville*, *valets de ville*, *gardes*, *gardiens*, or whatever else local tradition chose to call them) were to serve under him was left to local government. The police of Paris went through a variety of changes during the Revolution until, in 1800, the Prefect of Police was created, a position not greatly dissimilar to the old *lieutenant général* and with an equally large remit to supervise the city.

The Directory, the regime which ran revolutionary France from November 1795 to November 1799, established a ministry of police to co-ordinate matters of police across the republic. In September 1799 the post was given to Joseph Fouché, a former schoolmaster for the Oratorian Order and then a Jacobin extremist. Fouché continued in the post throughout most of Napoleon's rule.

Exercise   Early in 1800 Fouché put forward to General Bonaparte, then a Consul, proposals for reorganizing the police of Paris. You will find an extract from his comments as Document I.15. Read it now, and note how Fouché is seeking to shift the definition of police.

Discussion   Fouché is seeking to differentiate between government administration and police. He regards the police as an instrument of government, rather than of the administration in general or of the aims of that administration. Moreover, while the administration should be open and under the public's gaze, the actions of the police should be secret.

Fouché's stress on secrecy might have made you think in terms of political policing, though this is not precisely articulated here. Nevertheless, as minister of police, Fouché did run a formidable intelligence-gathering organization receiving information from the *commissaires*, and from other agents, across the empire, and acting upon it. Fouché's police do not appear to have been especially brutal, and relatively few political offenders were executed during his tenure. His problem, as far as Napoleon was concerned, was that he was too clever. Napoleon never really trusted Fouché and established rival intelligence organizations in the army and in the Paris Prefecture. He dismissed Fouché in 1810 for having developed links with the British government, but the wily old policeman had the last laugh by coming back, albeit briefly, as Louis XVIII's minister of police. The system of collecting a wide range of general information (*renseignements généraux*) relating to the state and its population, which had been developed under Fouché, continued to be pursued within the French police, and was employed elsewhere on continental Europe. Less able, and less subtle police ministers combined it with, at best harassment, at worst brutality and the employment of *agents provocateurs*. The Restoration period provided several examples of such as police chiefs, notably the Prince of Canosa in Sicily and the Paris Prefect of Police Guy Delavau both of whom set out to crush societies like the *Carbonari* and various forms of liberalism.

While eighteenth-century enlightened despots had sent men to study French police methods, Napoleon's armies brought those methods to Europe. The gendarmerie offers perhaps the best example of this. During the old regime the Piedmontese government had sent the occasional military expedition into the mountains to suppress banditry. Piedmont was incorporated into Napoleon's empire and the small, permanent brigades of gendarmes stationed in the towns and villages were instrumental in bringing Piedmontese banditry to an end. When the empire collapsed and the house of Savoy was restored to Piedmont, King Victor Emanuel I and

Figures 2 and 3
*The roles of the rural police. These illustrations from the popular press of 1899
portray the Carabinieri of the Italian state in heroic mould. On the left, they are
shown assisting the local population of Salerno during the floods of October 1899;
on the right, a patrol is shown in action against Maffiosi in Trapani, Sicily. Note
where we (the viewers) are in these illustrations. In the first case we are with the*

people looking out for help from the Carabinieri. In the second we are behind the Carabinieri being protected from the Maffiosi. Obviously you would need to analyse many more such illustrations before drawing any hard and fast conclusions, but there is at least something here for you to think about in these portrayals of these representatives of the new Italian state. (From: Dalla Cronaco alla Leggenda, Fratelli Spada, 1990. Copyright: Fratelli Spada S.p.A.)

his ministers resolved to sweep away everything French, except the gendarmerie now called the *Carabinieri*. Cardinal Consalvi, the chief minister of the restored Papal States, had been a vigorous opponent of Napoleon, yet in 1816 he established the Papal *Carabinieri* based on the French model.

The Napoleonic wars had helped to foster banditry and brigandage in different parts of Europe; there were deserters from the armies which crossed and recrossed Europe, young men who had avoided conscription, and others thrown out of work by the economic war which Britain and France chose to fight and which affected much of the continent. Gendarmes could therefore be proclaimed by the national governments as the men who would protect people from bandits, beggars and vagabonds. But other reasons can be suggested for the development of these military-style police. The gendarmes were representatives of the state, and the small barracks – the homes for brigades of four to six men – with the national flag flying over them, were visible manifestations to the peasantry that they lived in a nation state. The gendarmes were present in the countryside to protect the population, but they were also there to ensure that the population paid its dues to the state – young men for conscription, and taxes. The point to remember is that many of the states were relatively new in 1815 – Baden, Bavaria and Württemberg had all been created during the Napoleonic period – and others were restored. Napoleon's empire, though it had been defeated, still provided the administrative and legal model for many of these states; and in the countryside the gendarmes became the physical embodiment of the law.

What you have just read about gendarmeries is an interpretation – as it happens it is my interpretation (Emsley, 1993). One of the criticisms which can be levelled against this interpretation is that it is impossible to put together a set of documents from each of these countries in which ministers and their bureaucrats write about the need to create a gendarmerie to show the flag in the countryside, to be the physical manifestation of the law, both to protect the people and to ensure that they pay the reciprocal obligations of conscripts and taxes. Does that invalidate my interpretation? Or is it naive to expect that you have to find a document to support every interpretation? Do documents give *the answers*, or are they opaque in as much as you have to look at them with considerable care, and fill in lots of gaps? I want to explore this further by looking at the development of the English police in the early nineteenth century.

Throughout the eighteenth century the English had been suspicious of the idea of police. The word was rarely used and continental European notions of a *Polizeistaat* with responsibility for *Sicherheit* and *Wohlfahrt* was anathema. There was an idea which cut across social divisions that England was a land of liberty in contrast to continental Europe where the monarchs were absolutist and where the populations were held in thrall by Catholicism. Police organizations were regarded as inimical to English liberty since they were composed either of spies or of soldiers. Writing in the early 1760s Sir William Mildmay, an Englishman resident in Paris, was full of praise for the efficiency of the police of Paris and the *maréchaussée*; but he also recognized their military nature which meant that they could not 'be initiated by our administration, under a free and civil constitution of government' (Mildmay, 1763, p.vi).

The French Revolution and the subsequent Napoleonic regime tended to confirm many in these prejudices. Following two multiple family murders in the East End of London in 1811 the Early of Derby could write:

> They have an admirable police at Paris, but they pay for it dear enough. I had rather half a dozen people's throats should be cut in Ratcliffe Highway every three or four years than be subject to domiciary visits, spies, and all the rest of Fouché's contrivances. (quoted in Philips, 1980, p.174)

But others were becoming anxious, especially in London. It was the largest city in Europe with about a million inhabitants. There were some districts with appalling slums; there had been intermittent popular disorder in the city, and the French Revolution had given an awful warning of the danger from crowd violence even in 'well-policed' Paris. Some changes had been implemented before the end of the eighteenth century. Several parishes had significantly improved their system of night watchmen; some half a dozen police offices each staffed by three magistrates and a few constables had been established, and the most famous of these offices, that in Bow Street, had men patrolling beats on several main roads.

Exercise   Read Documents I.16, I.17 and I.18 and answer the following questions.

1   Why did the 1818 select committee reject the idea of establishing a police force? and where have you seen such ideas expressed before?

2   The extract from the 1828 select committee's report deals with one particular branch of policing: what is it? and what's wrong with it?

3   What did Peel identify as the problem? and how did his analysis of the cause differ from that of the 1818 committee?

4   What sort of statistics did Peel use? and can you think of any problems in assessing crime rates from these statistics?

5   Given the improvements which Peel felt might be facilitating crime, and noting the places where he argued crime was increasing and where decreasing, can you think of any other contradictions in his argument?

Specimen Answers 1   They considered such a force to be incompatible with a free society. This was an argument in the tradition of Mildmay in the 1760s and Derby in 1811.

2   The watch. The problem is that there is no unified system of organization and control, and this leads to problems even where the watch are efficient.

3   The problem was rising crime in London. The 1818 committee considered that manners and morals were improving, implied that increasing crime was the result of distress, and put its faith in education. Peel, in contrast, considered crime to be the work of 'trained and hardened profligates'.

4   He used the numbers of people committed for trial to prove the increase in crime. That, to put it generously, is decidedly dubious. Even today with the statistics of crimes reported to the police there are problems (what, for example, about crimes not reported, how can you measure them?). If you only count the number of people arrested and charged, you might be able to say something about the efficiency

of the system of policing (and it is a very big 'might'), but it is difficult to know how this can be used as a measure of increasing crime. More committals might mean better police rather than more crime – in which case Peel's evidence contradicts the case he was making. The point is that crime statistics were in their infancy during this period, and committals going back to 1805 were the only ones available.

5   Peel identified the biggest problem of increasing crime as being in London, and he contrasted the committal statistics there with those of Lancashire and Yorkshire. He then went on to suggest that the recent mechanical improvements which were bringing prosperity to the country were also facilitating crime. Yet were not Lancashire and Yorkshire centres of the new processes of industrialization where you might expect to find more of these mechanical improvements than London?

Peel got his police force for London in 1829. The old system of watchmen was abolished, and subsequently so too were the constables in the offices like Bow Street. Peel has received a good press from traditional historians of the police; they have accepted the argument that crime was rising and that the police were the solution. Manifestly the 1818 committee did not think that a police force was the solution; so was that committee wrong and Peel right? Do we not rather have to probe for the assumptions behind their assertions – if you like, to look for the 'unwitting testimony'? Perhaps the unwitting testimony of the 1818 committee is more apparent than that of Peel's speech; and that of the 1828 committee is even more explicit – note their 'presumption ... even though they had had no evidence as to particular facts'. Other evidence shows that, as home secretary from the early 1820s, Peel had been determined to reform and reorganize the criminal justice system. He had rationalized much of the criminal law by the middle of the decade, and from the beginning he had police reform on his agenda. It appears that both he and certain other Tories, notably the Duke of Wellington, initially contemplated some sort of nationwide police system; but in the end they had to make do with a police for the metropolis – and even there they had to exempt the square mile of the City of London which could call on considerable voting power in parliament, and had no intention of losing its distinct identity and privileges. The point to remember is that even though the evidence shows Peel telling parliament in 1829 that crime was increasing and that therefore he wanted to establish the Metropolitan Police, Peel's aims and the meaning of the statistics which he used were both much more complex.

In the early 1830s the new, reforming Whig government also discussed the possibility of introducing legislation to establish a national police. They eventually rejected the idea on the grounds of expense and the unlikelihood of getting such a measure through parliament – not only was there the long-standing English hostility to police, but they recognized that the gentry, who were responsible for local government in the counties, would object vigorously to any such centralizing measure. However, the Whigs did put clauses in the Municipal Corporations Act of 1835 requiring the creation of police forces in corporate boroughs, and they introduced enabling legislation for the creation of county police forces in 1839 and 1840. Not all municipal corporations implemented the police requirements of the 1835 act; and not all counties took up the enabling legislation. In 1856, however, new legislation compelled them to do so. The latter was the work of a government determined to establish some system of policing across the whole country; yet it had to make concessions to get the legislation passed including dropping the requirement that the smaller borough forces amalgamate with their larger county neighbours and the promise of an annual treasury grant for 'efficient' forces. 'Efficiency' was to be assessed annually by three, new officials, Her Majesty's Inspectors of Constabulary. The successive acts led to three distinct forms of police force in England and Wales.

1   The Metropolitan Police of London, whose chief officers were answerable directly to the home secretary. The fact that, though they contributed to the cost of the police, they had no say in its management, continued to be a bone of contention with local government in London.

2   The borough police, whose head constables were answerable to the borough watch committees; these committees were appointed by the elected representatives on the town councils.

3   The county police, whose chief constables had more autonomy than their borough counterparts, being responsible to both the home secretary and local government – before 1888 the latter meant the county magistrates, afterwards it meant standing joint (police) committees of magistrates and elected county councillors.

A largely similar structure was created by legislation in Scotland, but the other part of Great Britain – Ireland – witnessed the development of a different form of policing. The Dublin Metropolitan Police was, in many respects, similar to the London force; there was no local government control or supervision. Outside Dublin Ireland was patrolled by the Royal Irish Constabulary; another national force responsible only to a national government. The RIC was armed and barracked like the French gendarmerie. Also like the national police in France, both the Dublin force and the RIC had political departments.

Many European Liberals, who already felt a considerable attraction for things English, urged the development of police forces for their own countries along the lines of their perception of the English police. It was not lost on these Liberals that England, with its unarmed, civilian police escaped revolution in 1848, and they attempted to equate the two. Hamburg, for example, was ruled by an elected Senate which generally considered England as a model of liberty and it tried to model its police on the London Bobby; the lax censorship which resulted infuriated the Prussians who sent their own police agents into the city after 1848. An Italian parliamentary commission of the early 1860s considered England as the 'classic land of liberty'.

   ... the use of passports is unknown, no one ever asks the name of an individual, there are neither secret expenses nor secret agents; the guards are armed only with a small club. And yet that police ... can be said to touch perfection in the cities, and can be said to be the administrative masterpiece of Sir Robert Peel! The policeman answers for the security of people and property. For all its vigilance and courage in the repression of crime it is equally commendable for being benevolent, kind, and concerned for the interests of the community. (quoted in Hughes, 1987, p.120)

But the old ideas of police continued among the crowned heads of continental Europe and their ministers. Police still had its twin functions of *Sicherheit* and *Wohlfahrt*. You will remember from Unit 3 how the bureaucratic police of Imperial Germany and Imperial Russia had considerable regulatory control over their respective populations. Increasingly, however, much of the old welfare function was assumed by other bureaucratic functionaries and the police were left more and more with security, in the widest sense, as their principal tasks.

Even Napoleon III sought to introduce elements of the London Police system into the Paris police when he set about their reorganization at the beginning of the Second Empire. Adopting elements of the Metropolitan Police model suited well with his Liberal posturing.

In spite of his liberal pretensions Napoleon III believed that his police should maintain a strict surveillance of his political opponents. The *commissaires spéciaux de chemins de fer* (special *commissaires* of the railways), established as a national group in the 1840s for policing the developing railway system in France, became almost entirely politically oriented in the 1850s. In Prussia at the same time the Police President of Berlin, Carl Ludwig von Hinckeldy, a close confidant of the king, was given the responsibility for all security matters in the kingdom; an attempt to make him responsible for all kinds of policing in Prussia was blocked by other sections of the state bureaucracy jealous of their own authority. Alongside the increasing development of political police in the different states after 1848, these police also began exchanging information with each other across national frontiers on a more formal basis.

Exercise   Two countries remained noticeably apart from the development of political police: Britain (excluding Ireland) and Switzerland. (A word of warning: I am not saying that there was *no* political surveillance in Britain – Chartists and others were watched and infiltrated – but the scale and intensity of political policing in Britain was quite different.) Can you think of any reasons discussed above, or earlier in the course, why Britain was different in this way. (I don't expect you to come up with any suggestions regarding Switzerland, but if you can, fine!)

Discussion   It is always difficult to show why the political developments apparent in one set of countries did not happen in others; states manifestly do not follow identical paths. However in thinking about this question it is worth considering the following:

1   The traditional hostility to policing, particularly when it appeared to involve spies, in England. This, as I noted above, was something which spread across the social divides – members of the government, who would have been responsible for establishing political police, shared such beliefs.

2   The fact that Britain did avoid revolution in 1848, and its relatively stable constitutional structure during the nineteenth century. In most

other states there were political groups waiting in the wings with alternative constitutions and posing a potentially serious threat to existing governments. In Britain, however, the Chartists, who did take to the streets in 1848, did not demand a *new* constitution; rather they wanted to be incorporated within the old one.

3   The British believed that they were a land of liberty where political police were unnecessary. They allowed refugees from the political police of other countries to seek asylum on their shores, notably after the revolutions of 1848 (Karl Marx worked daily in the same seat in the Library of the British Museum for years); they maintained a very loose surveillance of the more extreme of these, and were reluctant to co-operate with the police of other European states over such matters.

The Swiss had a similar ideology to the British, regarding themselves a land of liberty and allowing political refugees to find sanctuary among them. Switzerland was also a federal state and it would have been very difficult to persuade all of the cantons either to accept a federal political police, which ran counter to ideas of liberty, or to agree to set up linking systems of political police across the whole country.

Change was eventually forced on both Britain and Switzerland by pressure of events. In the late 1860s and again in the early 1880s Britain was hit by Irish terrorism. The second of these bombing campaigns led to the creation of the Metropolitan Police Special Branch – originally the Special Irish Branch. At roughly the same time both the British and the Swiss governments found themselves under pressure from their neighbours to take action against some of the political refugees who had taken asylum in their territories. These refugees included Anarchists and Nihilists who were fully prepared to use assassination and terror to achieve their ends. In 1878 there were two attempts on the life of the German Emperor. Three years later Tsar Alexander II was killed by the bombs of a group calling itself *Narodnaya Volya* (the People's Will). Johann Most, a German Anarchist resident in London, published an essay in the Anarchist journal *Freiheit* (Freedom) applauding the assassination and trusting that it would provide the model for others. Under pressure from Berlin the British government prosecuted Most and then the staff of *Freiheit*. Britain was a great power and rather less easy to push around than Switzerland. The latter found herself under even stronger pressure to stop being a political asylum; she also found herself the unwelcome host to secret police agents from other powers.

Much of the history written about European police during the nineteenth century has concentrated on their political role. Yet while security in its broadest sense was given increasing predominance in police duties, political supervision played a relatively small part in the day-to-day tasks of men patrolling the city streets or country roads.

Exercise   Read document I.19 and answer the following questions:

1   What does *Commissaire* Pélatant consider to have been wrong with the old French police?

2   What does he consider should be essential to the men in the modern police?

3   In what ways does this extract from Pélatant differ in its assessment of the police from the ideas of Fouché?

Specimen Answers   1   Pélatant describes the old police as using spies, and exercising arbitrary and sometimes brutal authority.

2   New policemen should be prepared for criticism, should operate openly, and be prepared for hard work and self-sacrifice. In many respects he might be said to regard policing as a vocation.

3   Fouché believed that the police should operate secretly as the arm of government. Pélatant, in contrast, believed that all police activity should be open. He considered the police role to be the maintenance of order, rather than simply the maintenance of the government, and the protection of the weak. In a society of citizens, aware of their dignities and rights, the only individuals who should be in awe of the police were, in Pélatant's estimation, offenders.

Pélatant stands out as a reformer. He was a professional bureaucrat who had completed a thesis at Dijon on police organization in 1899. His appointment to Grenoble as *Commissaire Central* in 1903 was his first post, and no doubt the local municipality began to wonder what had hit them when the annual reports of their new police chief contained lengthy discussions on the theoretical aspects and nature of policing. Yet in other ways Pélatant was typical of a new kind of police ethos in France, rather more in the liberal (and in some respects the English) mould. For ten years before Pélatant's appointment to Grenoble, Paris had experienced a relatively enlightened, progressive police administration under Prefect Louis Lépine.

Elsewhere in Europe towards the end of the nineteenth century and beginning of the twentieth, there were similar attempts by central authorities and by senior officers to make their policemen appear more professional and more acceptable. In Italy the police authorities emphasized their professionalism and expertise in the way that they stressed their use of the new criminological theories. In Prussia the government continued to stress the military nature of its police, but it also projected an image of bureaucratic and legal correctness; such behaviour, it was believed, would enable the police to transcend any class differences in the state and to be regarded as vigilant guardians of the law and protectors of the weak. The extent to which the legitimate force of the different states, as manifested by their police forces, was accepted by the peoples of the states, is the question to which I want now to turn.

People's force versus legitimate force

Exercise   Read Documents I.20 and I.21 and answer the following questions.

1   What sort of document is Document I.20?

2   What events does it describe?

3   Who do the gendarmes criticize for not siding with them?

4   Do you see any similarities between the contents of the two documents?

Specimen Answers   1   A police report.

2   An attempt by a squad of gendarmes to apprehend some deserters, and the resulting disorder.

3   The mayors of the two villages and, less explicitly, the local *curé*.

4   They are both police reports dealing with popular disorder; and in both instances that disorder focuses in part on the police.

What these two documents give us are examples of popular force being used against the 'legitimate' (in the state's definition) force of the policemen.

Exercise   Do the crowds described in these documents appear to be just dangerous mobs out for plunder?

Discussion   Well they were pretty dangerous if you happened to be a policeman (though in neither instance does anyone appear to have been seriously injured). But you do not usually expect mayors and *curés* to be involved with mobs. In the French example the crowd was determined to protect refractory conscripts; the disorder only started when the various subterfuges of false names and lost birth certificates had failed. In the English example the hostility was initially directed against a group of gamekeepers following four poaching cases (and perhaps the police were expecting trouble given that they had provided an escort). The disorder then spread to an attack on the house of the gentleman who owned the land on which the poaching had occurred.

Legally, of course, the crowds could not have justified their actions; but they probably did consider that they had a case. Conscription during the Napoleonic wars was greatly resented; the state might have considered that it was the duty of every young Frenchman to serve in the armed forces, but not every young Frenchman saw it like that, and nor did their communities, especially in the more primitive parts of France, such as the

Pyrenees, where the incident reported in the document occurred. While not every poacher was a poor man seeking to find food for his starving family, the game laws aroused great hostility in Britain for much of the century. A variety of other laws and requirements by the state prompted individuals and communities to oppose their force to that of the police, or army – new forestry laws, which circumscribed or abolished traditional customs of seeking firewood, new poor law regulations, new taxation, are just a few examples.

There has been considerable research by historians into crowd behaviour. E.P. Thompson, studying what he called 'the moral economy of the eighteenth-century crowd', concluded:

> It is possible to detect in almost every eighteenth-century crowd action some legitimising notion. By the notion of legitimation I mean that the men and women in the crowd were informed by the belief that they were defending traditional rights or customs; and, in general, that they were supported by the wider consensus of the community. (Thompson, 1991, p.188)

This idea has been developed by an American historian, John Bohstedt, who suggested that in some instances rioting might be best understood as community politics. It involved the poorer members of society acting to bring to the attention of their social superiors a situation which was regarded as a problem or offensive; ritual played a significant part in the disorder, violence was limited, and even though the disorder was commonly characterized as a 'riot' people were rarely seriously hurt. The most common cause of rioting (or at least the most commonly researched by historians, and the problem of counting riots is similar to that of counting crimes) seems to have been food shortages or high prices. As the liberal ideas of the market economy replaced a more traditional paternalism, this kind of disorder may have become more violent since it was less likely to get a result. Also, Bohstedt suggests, as towns and workplaces grew bigger, thus distancing social classes, and as employers were less inclined to mix with their workforce, so the potential for violence increased (Bohstedt, 1983).

But the disorders noted above were essentially reactive, and in western Europe at least, after roughly 1850, food riots greatly diminished as national and regional economies expanded, became more integrated with each other and less dependent on their own immediate resources. While, again, it is difficult to count the number of incidents, it is probably true to say that as the nineteenth century progressed there was an increase in the number of pro-active actions on the part of the new working class in the form of strikes.

These were rarely violent at the outset, but they could become so. The problem for the strikers was to maintain solidarity and to prevent others from taking their place; this could be done by a variety of methods from picketing to violent intimidation. Drawing a legal line between peaceful picketing and obstruction could be very difficult; and while strikers might want to prevent what they considered to be blackleg labour from working, the police could be instructed to permit free labour to make its way, unhindered to the place of work. Small wonder then that strikes could witness violent confrontations between strikers and police, with the latter sometimes backed by troops; small wonder also that the police could become extremely unpopular.

Exercise   Read Document I.22. What is the problem, do you suppose, for the state's law and authority outlined in this document?

Discussion   The local men commonly engage in fights, but they prefer to resolve arguments and injuries by personal, financial arrangements. The mayor disapproves of the locals' disorderly habits; but with regard to the state's law, in theory, disorders, and injuries resulting from assaults or rights, should be settled in the state's courts.

At the beginning of the nineteenth century peasants across Europe were prepared to use the courts to deal with matters of land tenure, customary rights, feudal obligations and so forth; they might also use the courts in matters of theft and assault, but with the latter cases, the courts were often a place of last resort because they were expensive and took time. Much of what we might term common crime in a peasant village or small town – theft or assault – was just as likely to be resolved by negotiation involving the victim and the offender, their friends, and some person of authority – the local mayor, priest or notary. There were exceptions. In southern Europe assault (either physical, or verbally directed against an individual's 'honour') and the appropriation of goods or property (what, in some instances, the law might term 'theft') could generate a blood feud within the community. Statistically the most violent region of nineteenth-century France was the remote, relatively poor and backward island of Corsica where some feuds lasted the length of the century. In many peasant regions of Europe offences involving outsiders to the community, or which were regarded as particularly serious, might be settled by shaming or violent communal punishment. A petty thief could be roughed up and have part of his head shaved; a horse thief – and since horses were of particular value in a peasant community, their theft was consequently regarded as particularly serious – could be lynched. In Russia such practices were known as *samosud* – judging by oneself.

From the point of view of state jurists and administrators *samosud*, and its equivalents elsewhere in Europe, were demonstrations of the peasant's lack of civilization. The men at the centre of government wanted to put an end to such behaviour; their gendarmes and their policemen were the representatives of the law and the only individuals authorized to employ force against offenders. But change does not appear to have happened purely and simply because the men at the centre willed it. Increasingly the leaders of village and small town communities distanced themselves from their poorer neighbours and were no longer available for resolving disputes and petty offences. The Mayor of Teyssieu would be a good example here. His predecessors of a generation or so earlier would have been the kind of men to negotiate resolutions to thefts and violence – rather like the mayors of Segura and Malliou who were prepared to back reluctant conscripts against the gendarmerie. As it became more difficult to find responsible men in the community to resolve such problems, it seems probable that people turned more to the representatives of the state and its law to do so; this, in turn, gave increasing authority to those representatives and to the law. But there were notable exceptions as we will discuss in the next section.

Gentry authority versus state authority

Exercise   Above in the section entitled 'Police and gendarmerie', I noted that Peel decided not to try to impose the Metropolitan Police on the City of London and that the Whig government rejected the idea of a national police in the early 1830s. What was common to these decisions?

Discussion   In the case of the Metropolitan Police Peel did not want to antagonize the City which had significant power in parliament; and while it was only one reason for the Whigs' rejection of the idea of a national police, they feared the hostility of the county gentry to a centralized police. We might say, therefore, that in both instances the government's decisions were shaped by the desire not to run into conflict with powerful vested interests.

Elsewhere in Europe the extent of the power of lords and gentry played a significant role in the development of national police. In Ireland the gentry aspired to the same power and independence as their English counter-parts. But whereas, during the late eighteenth and the first half of the nineteenth century, the English gentry had shown themselves vigorous as magistrates acting to limit bread riots, recruiting riots, Luddism, Chartist disorders, and such like, in Ireland the gentry had appeared supine and ineffective against riot and rebellion. While they protested, the Irish gentry had little power to influence either the parliament at Westminster or the administrative authorities in Dublin Castle and they failed to prevent the creation of a centralized gendarmerie force to cover the whole country. Prussia provides a sharp contrast. The Junkers of East Prussia had con-siderable power and authority. While loyal to their kind, they intensely disliked the royal gendarmerie which had been created in 1812. They saw it as undermining their paternal authority over the peasantry on their estates. According to the nobles of Brandenburg the new police were inter-fering in what was essentially a family relationship between Junker and peasant: 'the police must not involve themselves in private and family rela-tionships unless those relationships collide with the state or its security' (quoted in Berdahl, 1988, p.143). In 1820 the Junkers succeeded in getting the gendarmerie significantly reduced in size, and while they lost some of their local police powers in the revolutions of 1848, they kept others until the end of the First World War. The monarch in southern Germany had similar problems with traditional authority resenting the advance of the power of the state in the form of its police. In Württemberg, for example, throughout the restoration years the cities, which had been largely independent before the Napoleonic period, resisted the spread of the monarch's new police as an encroachment on their prerogatives. But it was in southern Italy where such resistance was most serious for the state and had the most pronounced long-term effects.

   While the French had been successful in suppressing banditry and brigandage in the north of Italy – and the restored monarchy of

Piedmont, with the backing of the local nobility, maintained a French-style gendarmerie after the Restoration – they failed in the south. But then, economically and socially, the south of Italy (or the *Mezzogiorno* as it is commonly called) was a much more fertile territory for brigandage than the north. Communications in the south were poor; there was simply no network of roads. Brigandage in Calabria profited from the opportunities for smuggling British goods during the Napoleonic period – the goods came from Sicily where Ferdinand, the Bourbon King of Naples, had taken refuge under British protection. Brigandage also profited from the changing structure of agriculture. Enclosure, deforestation and cereal crops were threatening the old pastoral economy, and in particular the annual movement of sheep from the mountains to the plain. The brigands were often supported, sometimes even organized by those with large investments in sheep and grazing; they lived openly in the villages under the protection of their powerful patrons. But the brigands were not just the tools of the powerful; they used the opportunities of playing one patron off against another. They also relied on the strong bonds of kinship and clan identity in the region; though this did not prevent them oppressing the poor as well as the rich. In Sicily the brigands were more clearly the descendants of feudal retainers. From the late seventeenth century many of the large landowners were ceasing to live on their lands and were contracting large leaseholders (known as *gabelloti* from the form of lease contract). The *gabelloti* were drawn from the better-off peasants who, themselves, had some land, from the estate managers, tax-collectors, and local field guards (*campieri*). The *gabelloti*, in turn, sub-leased to the less well-to-do forming a pyramid of patronage; authority within the network was enforced by violence. In western Sicily the *gabelloti* and their clients became deeply involved in rustling for the meat market in Palermo; and as they spread into the city they needed compliant butchers, agents to deflect officialdom, and/or officials ready to turn a blind eye.

Restored to power on the fall of Napoleon, the Bourbon monarchy failed to make much impression on brigandage in either Sicily or Calabria. Unification initially made the problem worse for, in addition to the traditional brigandage there were thousands of disbanded Bourbon troops and *Garibaldini* wandering through the southern countryside, and there was peasant resentment at the introduction of conscription. But unification meant that the full legitimate force of Liberal Italy could be brought to bear on the problem and there was a savage war against the brigands of the south. The armed brigands were outgunned by the army, but the system of clientage which had supported brigandage, especially in Sicily, was more difficult to deal with.

Exercise   Read Document I.23 and answer the following questions.

1   What does the Prefect identify as the problem in Sicily?

2   How does he characterize this organization?

3   How does his characterization fit in with my description of banditry in Bourbon Sicily?

Specimen Answers   1   Mafia.

2   A criminal organization which has an overall directing body.

3   My earlier description did not mention a criminal body directing things; rather it described a series of pyramids of clientage in which violence might be used both the enforce authority and to engage in rustling.

It has been popular to discuss 'the Mafia' as some kind of large criminal organization with an overall directing body. Prefect Soragni comes close to this in his report, though he seems to have much more understanding of the problem than others. In fact *mafia* – and the term only began to be used after unification – while it should be applied to male fraternities organized within Sicilian communities, was much the same as the pyramids of clientage running though rural districts and spreading into towns partly through cattle rustling; by the end of the century it had also come to infect the urban labour market. Prefects and *Carabinieri* might condemn *mafia*, so too might parliamentary enquiries, yet destroying the system of clientage was difficult. The government of united Italy failed, for a variety of reasons, to win the whole-hearted support of the Sicilian élite. The latter, in consequence, frustrated attempts to establish new town councils, new local police forces, and a new judicial system. Throughout the 1860s the Sicilian national guard proved unreliable when called on to support the national government. Soldiers and *Carabinieri* from the mainland were isolated from the Sicilian population and rarely spoke the same language; given the hard terrain and lack of roads in the interior, they rarely reached the scene of a disorder until it was long over. Gradually, however, the old system of clientage began to negotiate its way into the new nation state; the *gabelloti* expanded their properties when the state sold off church lands in the 1860s, they became local mayors, took other positions of authority, and by the end of the century were organizing electoral lists and voting. Legitimate violence and the potential violence of the local élites were thus fused as the clientage/*mafia* system seeped into the administrative and political structure of the nation state.

Legitimate force and gender

Exercise   Read Document I.24 and answer the following questions.

1   What, briefly, does the document describe?

2   What questions do you think you would need to pose so as better to understand these events?

Specimen Answers   1   A policeman accosts a prostitute and then apparently tries to have her arrested. The woman is injured, but eventually escapes by leaping into the river Rhône, where she is drowned.

2   Why exactly did the policeman accost her? What was his authority for calling for uniformed assistance to arrest her? Why was the woman so terrified? Was this a particular, isolated incident, or was it just an extreme example of others?

And, in addition to the story itself, you would also have to ask the usual questions of your source – what sort of newspaper was it? were such stories typical? what was its attitude to the police, the government etc.? Or do you believe everything you read in the papers (and in units)?

It would have been apparent to any contemporary Frenchman who read this story in 1876 that the plain-clothes policeman in the story was a member of the morals police – *la police des moeurs*. It appears to have been apparent to the prostitute who is reported as saying that she knew 'both him and his job'. The *police des moeurs* had its origins in the old regime, but it had developed considerably in the first half of the nineteenth century. Prostitution was not illegal, but it was subject to police regulation. Prostitutes were required to register with the police and to submit to regular medical examinations for venereal disease; if they were then found to be ill, they had to submit to treatment within the prison hospital. Failure to comply with these regulations, and working in a forbidden district could lead to arrest. But the arrest did not lead to a trial before any court of law, rather police officials could pass what were considered as administrative sentences to prison or hospital. There were problems with the system, but these affected young, working-class women rather than the system itself. It was, for example, possible for an arrest to be made on the grounds that a woman attempted to solicit a man by making a provocative look (*oeillade*). But the assessment of the provocative look was made by the policeman and the *commissaire* who took the necessary statements. Once the formal report was written the woman could become a prostitute simply because the morals police said so; it was a case of guilt by accusation. Periodically the police would secretly surround a district and conduct a *razzia*, or *rafle*, in which they gathered up all the women within that district.

Supporters of the system argued that it was progressive because the state was setting out to control the 'necessary evil' which existed to give release to the powerful sex-drive in men. The control was to ensure that the potential threats from prostitution to public health, to public morality and to public order were checked by careful supervision. This was not just a concern of the French, nor of the middle and upper classes. Morals police working under similar administrative regulations were established elsewhere, notably in Germany, Italy and Russia. In mid-century Britain there were calls for a similar organization and while these were rejected the Contagious Diseases Acts, operative in English garrison towns and seaports from 1864 to 1883, did give the police considerable power over prostitutes and, at the same time, put young, working-class women out on their own at night in danger of being labelled as such and arrested. Moreover, in some British towns and cities, such as Glasgow, the local élite constructed a control network centred on their local police, hospitals and Magdalene homes for reforming prostitutes. In some working-class districts the population disliked the traffic which prostitutes attracted, their behaviour in the streets and pubs, and the police attention. But there was also anger among those who felt themselves, or their daughters or wives at risk from officious policemen. Strong abolitionist campaigns developed in most countries, often prompted by stories like the one reported in the newspaper article from Lyon. These campaigns united politicians of the left, early campaigners for women's emancipation, and sections of the working class. It was not that these groups necessarily favoured prostitution as a way of life. The first two groups particularly saw the system of regulation as infringing the civil rights of women; and while they generally believed that women should have the freedom to choose their profession, they considered that improved education and employment opportunities would bring about an end to prostitution. It was, however, only in Britain that campaigning brought an end to what was, in any case, a rather less severe system.

This was taken by some as another example of the liberal nature of that country's police. 'The police-medical surveillance of prostitution', declared a Russia feminist in 1907:

> ... conforms to the despotic inclinations of the male sex and to their contempt for the human dignity of women. This connection is demonstrated by the fact that the Russia of serfdom was among the first countries to copy the French morals police ... [This system] has flourished in [Russia] the country of lawlessness and arbitrary power, while in England, a country of freedom and respect for the person, police regulation did not take root. (quoted in Engelstein, 1993, p.380)

Interpretations

Military history and the development of armies has long been a popular subject; the study of police is a much more recent concern of historians. It might be that armies have been seen as some form of embodiment of the nation state (remember Anderson's comments on pp.311–12 and noted at the beginning of this unit). The military fight for the state and therefore they figure prominently in official and/or patriotic histories. Policemen and gendarmes do not have a similar role. Their routine has tended to be mundane, as indeed has been much military routine; but the policeman's moments of success, or disaster, are less spectacular than those of the soldier, and have tended to be less central to the national history. Anderson stresses the increasing importance of military power to the nineteenth-century nation state; it is at least arguable that the development of the military machines and the scale of military spending could not have been achieved without a degree of order within the states, and that police and gendarmes were developed to establish and maintain that order. But, of course, interpretations differ.

In the first half of the century there were fears of 'the dangerous classes' – the term *les classes dangereuses* was coined in 1840 by Honoré Frégier, an official in the Paris Prefecture of Police, and it was rapidly taken up elsewhere. In Britain in the 1860s the term 'the criminal classes' was in vogue. There were dangerous people and there were criminal recidivists during the nineteenth century, but it would be hard to show that they were members of a 'class'. It would be even harder to show that they were primarily responsible for even a part of the violence in disorders, riots and revolutions during the century. A generation of historians have now accepted that revolutionary crowds were made up of ordinary people, and while there is debate about the concepts of 'legitimizing notions' and 'moral economy', few would dismiss them out of hand.

The traditional historians of policing accepted the arguments of nineteenth-century politicians, that the police were needed to repress increasing crime and disorder perpetrated by 'criminals', the dangerous classes and those who were duped or misled by political agitators. More recently it has been argued that the police were established, in England specifically, as 'domestic missionaries', to control and supervise the new workforce in the burgeoning cities (Storch, 1976). Besides the difficulty in demonstrating that crime and disorder were getting worse in the first half of the century, the problem for the traditional view is how can it take account of the legitimizing notions of many crowds, and accept the fact that much crime was the work of ordinary individuals from all walks of life who were not professional criminals or members of a criminal class? The view at the other end of the spectrum also has difficulties. How might it account for the demands for police from the working class, themselves increasingly the possessors of property in the nineteenth century and therefore vulnerable to theft and vandalism? How can it cope with the fact that working-class leaders were as much in favour of 'domestication', in the sense of good behaviour, sobriety and respectability, as any factory owner? And does it have any relevance beyond the relatively small industrialized and urbanized areas of nineteenth-century Europe, especially along the Mediterranean seaboard where clientage systems, with their own structures for maintaining authority and order, continued to exist and were gradually absorbed by the state?

References

Berdahl, R. M. (1988), *The Politics of the Prussian Nobility: The Development of a Conservative Ideology 1770–1848*, Princeton University Press, Princeton, N.J.

Bohstedt, J. (1983), *Riots and Community Politics in England and Wales 1790–1810*, Harvard University Press, Cambridge, Mass.

Dootjes-Dussuyer, I. (1979), 'Images de la Police et Opinion Publique: Une étude psycho-sociale des représentations sociales de la police dans le public', Thèse pour le Doctorat de Specialité (IIIe cycle) de Psychologie Sociale, Université des Sciences Sociales de Grenoble.

Emsley, C. (1993), 'Peasants, gendarmes and state formation', in M. Fulbrook (ed.), *National Histories and European History*, University College London Press, London.

Engelstein, L. (1993), 'AHR Forum: Reply', *American Historical Review*, 98, pp.376–81.

Hughes, S. C. (1987), 'Gendarmes and Bobbies: Italy's search for the appropriate police force', paper delivered at the Southern Historical Association Meeting, New Orleans.

Lüdtke, A. (1989), *Police and State in Prussia, 1815–1850*, Cambridge University Press, Cambridge.

Mildmay, Sir William (1763), *The Police of France: or, an Account of the Laws and Regulations established in that Kingdom for the Preservation of Peace and the Preventing of Robberies*, London.

Philips, D. (1980), ' "A new engine of power and authority": The institutionalization of law-enforcement in England 1780–1830', in V.A.C. Gatrell, B. Lenman and G. Parker (eds), *Crime and the Law: The Social History of Crime in Western Europe since 1500*, Europa, London.

Storch, R.D. (1976), 'The policeman as domestic missionary: Urban discipline and popular culture in Northern Europe, 1850–1800', *Journal of Social History*, 9, pp.481–509.

Thompson, E.P. (1991), 'The moral economy of the English crowd in the eighteenth century', in E.P. Thompson, *Customs in Common*, Merlin Press, London.

Unit 5
State and social policy

Prepared for the course team by David Englander

Contents

Study timetable

Weeks of study	Texts	Video	AC
2	Unit 5; Offprints 4, 5 and Charts 1–4; Document I.25; Anderson		

Aims

The aims of this unit are:

1   to outline the fundamental economic, political, ideological and institutional pressures for reform in France, Britain and Germany in the century after Waterloo;

2   to explore some possible connections between ideas and action and between social investigation and social reform;

3   to compare some of the ways in which patterns of governance adjusted to social policies within the political and organizational constraints of the period.

Objectives

By the end of this unit you should be able to:

1   specify the fundamental features of the development of social policy in France, Britain and Germany before 1914;

2   say how and why the social policy process differed between the aforementioned states;

3   appreciate some of the historiographical issues raised in the explanation of these differences.

Introduction

Advanced industrial societies are today characterized by a high level of government activity. A large part of their income is spent by their governments on a wide range of public and social services and a sizeable section of the labour force is employed by central and local government. How has this come about? Explanations of the transition from *laissez-faire* capitalism to welfare capitalism, or, if you will, from the liberal to the welfare state, are broadly of two kinds.

The 'progressive' school of historians see the expansion of social assistance and social protection as an innovative and benign movement from juridicial and civil rights to social rights, and from market-dominated values towards a needs-oriented and communally-centred public service ethic (Marshall, 1950). In this version, old age pensions, health and unemployment insurance are presented as important measures for the attainment of a significant re-distribution in the pattern of income and life chances.

Revisionist accounts, by contrast, interpret the expansion of welfare provision as a means of social control rather than social transformation. G.V. Rimlinger in a pioneering comparative analysis of the emergence of welfare systems in Europe and America concluded that they were conservative in intent, designed to correct imperfections in the market mechanism by re-allocating the costs of industrialization in a manner consistent with economic efficiency and social stability. Social insurance and attendant measures, it is argued, not only allowed workers to weather violent fluctuations in the domestic and international economy, they also improved labour productivity and cost competitiveness in world markets (Rimlinger, 1971). How satisfactory are these accounts?

Before we proceed to consider their merits, we need to clarify our terms. Welfare state means different things to different authors. Some scholars argue for a distinction between a 'social service state' characterized by minimal national standards of provision and a 'welfare state' defined by an explicit commitment to a comprehensive scheme of income maintenance and optimal level of service. On this basis the welfare state is very largely a post Second World War phenomenon. Others, by contrast, emphasize the use of taxation as a social instrument, and there is another school of thought which identifies shifts in social thinking as the essential criterion. What, from our point of view, is most interesting about these various definitions is their shared interest in the nature and purpose of public action.

Exercise   Look carefully at Chart 1 in your Offprints Collection. What similarities and differences can you identify in the character of state and social action in the nineteenth century?

Discussion   You might have concluded that, notwithstanding the differences in timing and method, all the states were moving towards increasing intervention to improve the welfare of their citizens. It certainly seems that way. Prussia passed factory acts in 1839 and 1853, introduced poor law reform in 1840 and health reform in 1852. France saw the passage of an educational act in

1841, factory legislation in 1841 and 1848, with poor law and public health reform in 1848 and 1850.

Industrialization, and the increased specialization and differentiation that came from it, unquestionably influenced the provision of social services. Industrialization, as Anderson notes (p.155ff.), led to migration from the countryside and the growth of towns; it changed family roles and relationships and made people dependent on paid employment for their livelihood; it required new forms of industrial training and created new health problems through an unregulated factory system and an unplanned process of urbanization. The state, it is sometimes argued, had to intervene to compensate for the failure of the traditional relief agencies – the family, church, guild and voluntary bodies – to cope with the resultant social problems. The response to industrialization was everywhere much the same with the exposure of abuse followed by the growth of bureaucracy. The welfare state, on this reading, is thus a necessary stage of societal development through which all industrial states must pass.

True or not, this interpretation does not explain how such changes came about. It does not explain why, for example, Germany which industrialized later than Britain, possessed the more advanced form of social insurance, or French priority in the adoption of a national system of primary education. Nor does it explain why women appear to have gained more from centralized authoritarian welfare systems than from liberal regimes. States had different origins and different traditions and different institutional and political frameworks into which social goals and objectives had to be fitted. The scope of public action was not simply a function of economic and social change. The historical, political and organizational structure of the state were equally as important in determining the nature of welfare provision. The contrasting forms of government, the different relationships between central and local government, the very heterogeneity of local government within the same country, meant that variety rather than uniformity ruled. The contrast between the centralized power of government in France and the federal constitution in Germany or the multi-national state in Britain, was reflected in the variable role assigned to government in the provision of welfare.

The exceptional character of the state form in mainland Britain – noted by Anderson pp.70, 73, 173–4 – is, for example, the function of a particular historical development. The agrarian élite that emerged victorious from the civil war of the seventeenth century was patrician rather than feudal or bourgeois in character, it monopolized political power and supplied the personnel and machinery of state. This ruling class created a tradition of informality, a personal, decentralized and non-bureaucratic form of control with a low-profile military, that set it apart from the impersonal, rational state forms discussed in Unit 2.

The transition from the patrician state to the 'nightwatchman state' – the minimal, regulatory *laissez-faire* state depicted by political economists – was accomplished without difficulty during the eighteenth and nineteenth centuries simply because it required no fundamental change in property relations. The nationalization of poor relief under central control, the creation of a factory inspectorate, growth of work-safety regulations and the assumption of overall responsibility for primary education in 1870, were not only in keeping with minimalist notions of public action, but were also implemented in a manner consistent with the interests of the landed aristocracy.

Ideas and institutions are also important. Ideas concerning the relations of the individual to the state, about the scope and functions of the state, were less developed in Britain than elsewhere. The notion of the state as the protector of society was deeply embedded in the assumptions and outlook of the French and the Prussians. The right of all citizens to work and the obligation of the state to protect the poor, included in the Declaration of the Rights of Man of 1793, gave Republican France a social purpose, which, though slow of fulfilment, was never forgotten.

Prussians had similar expectations. The community's duty to clothe and feed the worker incapacitated by age, infirmity or unemployment, was readily acknowledged. 'It falls to the state to make provision for the feeding and caring of citizens unable to provide their own upkeep or receive this from other private parties specifically liable for their provision under the law', said Prussia's General Law Code of 1794. 'Those who only lack the means and opportunity to earn their keep and that of their dependents', it continued, 'shall be given work suitable to their abilities and capacity.' A further provision which states that 'Those who from indolence, love of idleness and other slovenly tendencies show no desire to earn the means for their keep, shall be allocated useful work under appropriate supervision by coercive legal means and punishments', is, however, a striking reminder of the authoritarian and paternalistic character of the Prussian tradition of social action. The concept of *Polizeiwissenschaft*, which, as noted earlier, supplied the rationale for the integration of state welfare with social control (see Unit 3), continued to influence the thinking of large sections of German opinion, particularly among the employers and bureaucracy, throughout our period.

The British by contrast had no clear conception of the state and no coherent basis for the use of collective authority for social purposes. Nothing provides a more telling illustration of the poverty of social thought in Britain than the development of poor law policy. The Poor Law is important because it provided the institutional framework and principles for most publicly financed welfare provision in Victorian Britain. Until the passage of the Poor Law Amendment Act of 1834, the basis of social policy had rested with the Elizabethan legislation of 1601, which made it obligatory on the parish to provide relief and work. The Poor Law Amendment Act of 1834 abandoned this form of repressive paternalism in favour of a liberal conception in which the individual was free to pursue his or her fortune and in which success or failure was a matter of personal responsibility. The act of 1834 brought rigour and system to the management of the poor. The allegedly wasteful and irrational practices of the Old Poor Law, above all the misconceived promise of a living wage held out by the justices at Speenhamland, were swept away (see Chart 1, 1795). The new law perfected the system of the workhouses; henceforth the sick and the old were collected together in these institutions and outdoor relief prohibited. From that point on, the question of wages was entirely separate from that of charity; and the rate left to fluctuate in accordance with the law of demand and supply. The New Poor Law, in abandoning the Elizabethan legislation, reduced rather than enlarged the notion of the state's responsibility for the disadvantaged and the poor. Its narrowness was striking. Questions concerning the possible connection of social reform with broader social issues such as the improvement of labour force efficiency, or industrial adjustment to social needs and working conditions, were submerged beneath a preoccupation with poverty and its implications for local taxation. Attendant problems were dealt with in a piecemeal fashion; social reforms proceeded as though each item of legislation was a special case each with its own justification. No coherent image of Britain either as a social service state or as a welfare state emerged. The Poor Law Amendment Act, directed at the stratospheric rise in the cost of poor relief between 1770 and 1802, was first and foremost an economy measure. The wider implications of the Speenhamland decision for social policy were scarcely considered.

In truth, it makes more sense to think of the legislation of 1834 as the expression of a defensive strategy to relieve the landed interest of the cost of caring for the victims of economic and industrial change. To this end an aristocratic regime sanctioned the creation of a free-standing organization to work under the control of the legislature but independently of the machinery of local government. The three-man Poor Law Commission, set up to supervise the administration of the new law, despatched a number of assistant commissioners around the country to group parishes into poor law unions, assist the formation of boards of guardians and, where appropriate, to advise on the construction of new workhouses. By 1839 some 15,000 parishes had been grouped into 600 poor law unions and 350 new workhouses had been built. The new boards of guardians were elected on a narrow property-based franchise and their tax-powers were separated from those of the local authorities in order to discourage Speenhamland-style extravagance.

The argument as presented above is not without its difficulties. It implies a very coherent view of the state in France and Germany which some scholars will wish to question. It will also be objected that Benthamite reasoning about state institutions, which informed much of the arguments leading to the Poor Law Amendment Act of 1834, was probably the most precise yet abstract body of social thought one can locate in the first half of the nineteenth century. (Benthamite liberalism is discussed in Anderson, pp.339–40.) Moreover, the new legislation raised two other issues, apart from outdoor versus indoor relief: the units within which the poor were entitled to relief, and the rights of settlement and removal. These were problems which were addressed (and not in very dissimilar ways) in Prussia, for example, with various laws on poor relief and entitlement in 1842 (see Chart 4).

Against this, it may be argued that although the Benthamites had a rational concept of the state, they had no trust in democracy, little political skill and, in consequence, less influence in formulating an acceptable concept of the British state than might have been expected. Whether one should see the Prussian poor law reforms of the 1840s as a temporary deviation or a break with the dominant state paternalist tradition is, likewise, a moot point. All of this is to remind you that historians often disagree.

The variations displayed in our time chart not only reflect differences in decision-making procedures, ideology and timing, but are also a function of differing institutional capabilities. The key point to grasp is that, in terms of the growth and development of an effective centralized bureaucracy, Britain was the odd-man-out (Anderson, p.174).

So far we have concentrated upon differences and dissimilarities between states. Some of the patterns or common features will also have been identified. These are displayed more clearly in Chart 1, included in your Offprints Collection. In Chart 2 the information shown in Chart 1, is summarized by theme rather than by chronology. Let us examine Chart 2 more closely.

Education in Britain and France

france

Education, it will have been noted, was a priority for state action. In neither Britain nor France could it have been described as satisfactory. Schooling (i.e. the education of the poor) in nineteenth-century France was deficient in the towns and abysmal in the countryside. The rural schools that catered for the mass of the French population were ramshackle affairs housed in converted bakehouses, crumbling cottages, out-buildings etc., wanting in heating, toilets, teaching materials – in short, in everything that was conducive to effective learning. The quality of village teachers was about equal with the condition of the schools in which they taught. Before 1816 would-be teachers required no formal training or proof of competence. Anyone would do, and anyone did. Teaching might be no more than a form of secondary employment for the ex-soldiers, rural constables, barbers, grocers, and innkeepers from whom the instructors were often recruited. For much of our period it remained a low-status occupation. Peasants who were a dead loss in the fields, or who wished to avoid compulsory military service, took to teaching.

Britain

The British schooling system, though more responsive to the requirements of an industrializing economy, was left to voluntary agencies, Anglican and Nonconformist, or provided by private enterprise. By 1833 policymakers on both sides of the Channel were agreed that voluntary action unaided was unlikely to improve national efficiency or promote national integration. The British, though, backed off from the wholesale reconstruction of the educational system. The grant of £30,000 voted by the British parliament, in that year, the first allocation of public funds for the promotion of elementary education, looked meagre by comparison with the national system of state-aided primary schools created by François

Diff ⟶

Guizot, Louis Philippe's Minister of Instruction. It required every commune or group of neighbouring communes to establish and maintain a minimum of one elementary school; it endorsed the standards of competence for teaching embodied in the royal ordinance of 1816 and prohibited the operation of non-certified schools; it also required departments, singly or in combination, to create a normal school for the training of primary school teachers and created an inspectorate to see that standards were enforced. The results were impressive. In 1833 France had 31,420 schools attended by 1.2 million children; by 1847 the number of schools had doubled and the number of pupils increased threefold.

The British, by contrast, seemed laggardly. The allocation, voted in 1833 and renewed annually thereafter, was earmarked for school building and shared between the Anglican National Society and the undenominational British and Foreign School Society. France in 1848 had 47 normal schools at a time when the training and career structure of teachers in Britain was still in its infancy. Elementary education in Britain only became general in 1870, compulsory in 1876 and free in 1891. The question of a universal and free system of secondary education was postponed until after 1945.

Conflict between Anglican and Nonconformist undoubtedly delayed the introduction of a comprehensive system of public education. But it was not the only or most important consideration. The British, when finally they did move, created a highly stratified educational system in which the institutions of the privileged – the fee-paying grammar schools and public schools – were excluded from the reform effort. In France, where the religious quarrel was just as fierce, education became a civic religion and the very embodiment of the republican image of the state. Not for nothing was the Third Republic praised and described as *la république des professeurs*. Progress was considerable.

In 1881 all fees and tuition charges in public elementary schools were abolished, and in 1882 elementary education was made compulsory up to the age of fourteen. Apart from an expansion in school building and classroom resources public funds in the 1880s were also directed towards an improvement in the standing of the teaching profession. Salaries were raised and teachers encouraged to distance themselves from ordinary village folk, to dress suitably and adopt the ethos and bearing of the true *fonctionnaire d'Etat*. The prescribed role of the teacher as the agent of enlightenment and Republican virtue reflected the importance of state education as a source of national integration. Anderson, in a brief but useful discussion, notes that the demand for education was a market-led form of moral coercion designed to satisfy industrial and social requirements without disrupting the scheme of things. Guizot's moral force metaphor (cited in Anderson, p.170) with its emphasis upon state-building, underscores its peculiar strength in nineteenth-century France. France for much of the period covered in this course, was in many respects more a state rather than a nation. Its unitary structure notwithstanding, France was made up of various territories which had been conquered annexed and integrated in a political and administrative whole – many of them with pronounced national or regional identities, and some with traditions that were un-French or anti-French. Before the 1870s France possessed an administrative rather than a cultural unity; the rural masses were aware of the state but did not identify with it. Across vast tracts of the countryside standardized French was unknown; peasants spoke the language of the *pays* or in some equally incomprehensible dialect. An official inquiry of 1863 showed that some 7.3 million people, a fifth of the population, did not know the language. Metric measurement and the franc-based currency, too, were little used. In the hamlets and villages, where the bulk of people lived, there was wanting a sense of cohesion and commitment, an ideal of France as a national community with a particular perspective and an appropriate set of values to which allegiance might be given.

By 1914 the French people and the French state had come together. Apart from the drill sergeant and the road-builder, the chief agent of change had been the school teacher. Over the course of the previous generation schoolchildren had learned what the state did for them, why it imposed taxes and military service, and shown them how their true interests were bound up with those of the fatherland. The expanding school system, in short, transmitted not only the language of the dominant culture but also its values, above all the patriotism that was to sustain the French nation through the four bloody years that lay ahead. (The wider issues are taken up in Unit 12.)

Public health: comparisons and contrasts

Public health and housing reform likewise supplies a common theme for state action. Yet here again there are marked divergences to be explained. Take, for example, the development of French public health between 1800 and 1850. In the early nineteenth century France led the world in sanitary thought (Anderson, p.158). Social statistics and the application of knowledge for public benefit had been championed by the French Enlightenment. The complementary concept of the citizen-patient, developed during the Revolution, acknowledged the responsibility of the state for the health of the citizenry and the latter's obligation to look after themselves for the collective good. The philosophy of hygiene found systematic statement in the writings of Jean-Noel Halle while Villermé's careful investigations exposed the relations between morbidity, urban geography, occupation, poverty and culture. The pathology of the city, disclosed in Alexander Parent-Duchâtelet's extraordinary study of prostitution in Paris supplies a further indication of an intellectual framework of public inquiry that was well in advance of developments in Britain. Cohesion and commitment were reinforced though representation on the Royal Academy of Medicine and the Academy of Political and Moral Sciences and through the newly-created *Annales d'hygeine publique*. In the administrative sphere, public health councils were created in the principal cities to report on sweated trades and slaughterhouses.

Britain

The expected reconstruction of public health, though, did not happen. Londoners rather than Parisians became the first recipients of safe piped-water and main sewer drainage. From 1840 onwards the British extended public health provision, enlarged the powers of Medical Officers, enforced smallpox vaccination and introduced sundry measures of improvement. Edwin Chadwick, architect of the British system, considered the French laggards. The Paris Health Council was dismissed as a dead loss. 'The labouring population of Paris is shown to be, with all the advantages of climate, in a sanitary condition worse than the labouring population of London', he concluded. The enduring British image of the French

France

as a mucky lot owed something to the primitive sanitary arrangements that survived in town and country down to 1914 (Englander, 1994).

How can this be explained? Why, in spite of all the theorizing, was there so little in the way of concrete achievement? Contemporaries, then as now, often thought in terms of a 'French preference for uncleanliness'. Racial stereotypes, however, generate more heat than light, and should be avoided. Rather more convincing is the explanation advanced by Ann La Berge who suggests that, instead of looking for social transformation, we should attend to method rather than mission, to the creation of a new form of expertise in respect of health, wealth and society, a new status-bearing public health discipline from which the specialists were the principal beneficiaries. The French concept of *assainissement*, or sanitary reform, was quite unlike its British analogue. British social reformers, imbued with a utilitarian activism (which those who have studied A102 will well remember), believed that empirical evidence of poverty and inefficiency should be immediately translated into public policies. The French, by contrast, thought that the solution of environmental problems lay in personal effort and greater individual responsibility. Villermé's careful researches which, for example, showed that morbidity was the product of poverty or of vice, led to the conclusion that all attempts at legislation were inconsistent with the precepts of political economy and therefore futile.

why diff.

Housing strategies compared: Britain, France and Germany

Along with unemployment the housing question posed one of the most intractable of problems for state and local government in the urbanizing nations of nineteenth-century Europe. Attention has in general centred upon the problems of slum property and the ways in which policy emerged out of attempts to ameliorate the very worst conditions. Chart 3 (Offprints Collection) displays the salient features of this process.

Exercise   Study Chart 3 carefully and, in a few words, identify the key difference shown therein between Britain and other countries in relation to housing strategy.

Discussion   British legislation, it will be seen, proceeds from sanitary improvement and slum clearance to the assumption of responsibility for replacement housing and additional housing. French and German experience, by contrast, displays no unilinear progression towards state-subsidized housing as a solution to the housing problem. Housing policy in Paris and Berlin rested upon the use of money from insurance funds or savings banks to provide cheap loans to finance public housing programmes (Bullock and Read, 1985). Note, in particular, the terms of the German Invalidity and Old Age Insurance Act of 1890 which accounted for the provision of some 11,000 dwellings in Berlin before the First World War. Contrast the terms of the Housing of the Working Classes Act, passed by the British Parliament in 1890. How can these divergent strategies be explained?

Diss.

Space precludes a comprehensive comparison of housing strategies. Suffice it to say that historians have in recent years become increasingly sceptical of arguments that present the development of housing policy largely as a self-generating administrative response from slums to subsidies. Two aspects require attention:

- the pattern of landlord-tenant relations
- the differing relations between the state and the working class

We shall take each point separately.

Landlord and tenant

In Britain the tensions and conflicts generated by the operation of a free market in the provision, ownership and control of working-class housing, meant that the rights and obligations of the private landlord baulked larger in debates on housing strategy than elsewhere. High rents enforced by summary powers of eviction and the power to seize the possessions of defaulters to the value of the rent outstanding gave rise to the spread of tenants' defence associations and a growing demand for 'fair' rather than market-determined rents in the generation before the First World War. Tensions, though sharp in industrial England, were particularly acute on Clydeside where the onerous house-letting system (See House Letting and Rating Act, 1911, Chart 3) and endemic war between impoverished tenants and their landlords – there were over 20,000 evictions alone in Glasgow in 1906 – gave primacy to questions of protection and control (Englander, 1983). Whereas reformers in France and Germany regarded the private landlord as one of several providers of working-class housing within an integrated national programme, their counterparts in Britain were altogether more determined to exclude the private rented sector from public policy.

This turn towards state-subsidized housing was facilitated by the relative weakness of British property owners who lacked the political weight and national presence of their German counterparts. These differences in the situation of the German and British middle classes also reflect the pace of economic development. The slow growth of industrial capitalism in Britain left the petty bourgeois property owner tied to the ideology of *laissez-faire* whereas the small man in Germany, squeezed by the more rapid expansion of large-scale business, turned to the state for social protection. The weakness of small landlords within the British political system, both locally and nationally, is striking. There was nothing comparable in Britain with the Prussian three-class voting system (discussed in Anderson, p.1) which gave so much weight to property owners in state and local government. Owners of house property in Britain felt threatened by social reforming Liberals who hoped to pay for expensive welfare programmes by taxing land values, but found no security in a Conservative Party which seemed to have concluded that larger propertied interests might be better protected by the encouragement of owner occupation rather than by the continued support of the private rented sector.

State and working class

Equally important in determining the trajectory of German housing policy was the attitude of the labour movement towards the state. German *diff*

workers, unlike their British counterparts, saw the state as an expression of particular class interests, concerned with coercion and containment rather than a neutral agency that might act as an efficient provider of social services. German workers were, in consequence, much more inclined to develop autonomous trade unions and political associations to take advantage of the availability of cheap loans to build, own and manage their own houses and distance themselves from the state. The importance of class attitudes in the formation of social policy will be further explored in our discussion of British and German social insurance programmes in due course.

Social inquiry and social action

Britain

diff

In glancing through Chart 1 (Offprints Collection) you will have registered the importance of empirical social research, official and private, in mobilizing opinion in favour of particular remedies for social ills. Such activities were not, of course, unprecedented. The state from earliest times, had engaged in fact-finding research, usually for military and financial purposes. The Church, for so long the spiritual arm of the state, too had its visitations to assess resources and monitor personal conduct. Industrialization and urbanization made the need for more systematic information pressing, and this was reflected in a significant expansion of social inquiry both by government and voluntary agencies from the eighteenth century onwards. Variations in methods of inquiry again reflect significant differences in the political culture of the European states. In parliamentary democracies, like nineteenth-century Britain, it was expected that the testimony of the men, women and children who were the objects of investigation would be taken at first hand by the various royal commissions and select committees. In a bureaucratic state, like Germany, where people took little part in the affairs of government, such consultation was deemed unnecessary; investigation proceeded by means of *enquêtes* (questionnaire surveys) that were sent to officials and local dignitaries. Germany, too, was slower to develop a tradition of private inquiry comparable with that of the statistical societies that flourished across the North Sea and in Restoration France. The creation of the German Empire, however, gave a fresh impetus and a new agenda to private reform groups. The Social Policy Association in Germany, the Unions for Social Peace in France and the Booth Inquiry in Britain, were all private initiatives which preceded the introduction of new social legislation. Let us examine them more closely.

Germany

The contribution of the German professoriate to the national-building process in the *Kaiserreich* found its most practical application in the work of the Social Policy Association. The academics, drawn largely from political science and jurisprudence, met in general assembly every two years, to confer and submit specific policy recommendations to government and legislature. Their leading lights were Gustav Schmoller (1838–1917), Lujo von Brentano (1844–1931) and Adolf Wagner (1835–1917). Profoundly influenced by the work of the historical economists, Wilhelm Georg Friedrich Roscher (1817–94) and Karl Knies (1821–98) and their hostility to the abstract-deductive method of classical economics – or Manchesterism, as contemporaries called it – they set out to explore the singularities of real economic life as the basis for public action in lieu of the *a priori* assumptions of political economy. They came to be known, erroneously, as the *kathedersozialisten* or academic socialists. In fact, apart from professors, the Social Policy Association included a substantial cadre of administrators and large numbers of physicians, trade unionists, factory owners and other professionals. Chair-holders, like Schmoller and Wagner, who gave the Social Policy Association its tone and ethos, were conservative social reformers, close to the crown and ministers in the Prussian civil service.

Still, they were no slouches. One of the earliest meetings addressed deficiencies in the methods and machinery of the *enquête*, criticized the narrowness of the government's knowledge-base and the class bias inherent in the information-gathering process. The Association also concerned itself with the reform of apprenticeship, labour legislation and housing problems. Their conclusions were sometimes unexpected as with their support for socialist demands for freedom of association and the right to strike. Such radicalism, though, proved brittle. Under the impact of the anti-socialist legislation of the 1880s priorities were revised and research shifted away from the condition of the industrial worker to the comparatively 'safe' subject of the rural worker. The contribution of the *kathedersozialisten* to German social politics was nevertheless considerable. In the definition of the social question and in the mobilizing of opinion in favour of particular remedies it was important.

There was no equivalent of the Social Policy Association in France. Its contemporary, the Le Playist Unions for Social Peace, were different both in their theoretical perspective as well as in their research methods and agenda. Their founder, Frédéric Le Play (1802–82) was a mining engineer who was educated at the École Polytechnique. He became a professor at the École des Mines and served Napoleon III as a Conseiller d'Etat and Senator. He was conservative in outlook and neither very original nor penetrating. His thought proceeded from a belief in original sin and consequent antagonism to the 'false dogmas of '89' with their assumption of human perfectibility and the possibility of rule by natural laws. He believed that happiness rested on peace, stability and compliance with the Ten Commandments, and that the object of social inquiry was to identify the conditions and programmes that would best secure it.

In opposition to the ideas and doctrines of the French Revolution, he upheld a Catholic conception of morality, obedience and order. Social well-being, he argued, depended upon the degree to which these Christian principles were nurtured and sustained within families. These latter were of three kinds: the patriarchal family, in which property was held in common and transmitted from generation to generation; the stem family, in which one heir inherited all the land compelling the others to migrate, seek their fortunes, and make stem families of their own; and the unstable family, in which the erosion of family property and paternal authority militated against family continuity. Social peace, and progress, he believed, rested upon freedom of testation and the consequent strengthening of the stem family. Where such freedom had been retained, as with the Anglo-Saxon countries, prosperity, stability and opportunity were assured; where, as with Revolutionary France, it had given way to the forced partition of inheritance among heirs, the family as a moral and economic force had been fatally impaired.

In 1855 he published a volume of monographs dealing with working-class families under the title *Les ouvriers européens*, and a revised and enlarged edition in six volumes between 1877 and 1879. The work was based on extensive field trips at home and abroad undertaken over many years. Data was collected from eastern, northern and western Europe. Interviews, conducted with at least 300 individual families, ranged from the Bakshirs of Turkestan, to Parisian ragpickers and Sheffield knife-grinders. Families were observed under varying conditions, changing from simple to complex forms of social organization – from horse-power to steam-power, religious to secular, traditional to modern, and from the patriarchal and communal to the isolated and unstable family. Le Play restated and developed his ideas in various books and articles and through the monthly journal *La Réforme Sociale* which he founded in 1881 and which continued to give currency to his ideas until 1912.

Le Play's place in history, however, owes less to his preoccupation with the family as a key socio-economic indicator, and more to the innovatory investigative techniques he developed to study it. Like the leading lights of the Social Policy Association, he had little time for speculative or abstract social theory. As a metallurgist, he conceived of social science as an exercise in classification, a body of principles to be arrived at inductively after systematic comparison of observed social facts. In his own words: 'A mineral is known when the analysis has isolated each of the elements of its composition and when it has been verified that the weight of all these elements is exactly equal to that of the mineral. A numerical verification of the same sort is always available to the scholar who analyses the existence of the social unit constituted by the family'. The detailed breakdown of the budgets of income and expenditure, in his view, supplied the scientific precision necessary for meaningful social inquiry. 'Every fact about the existence of a worker's family ends up more or less directly in a receipt or an expenditure', he remarked. 'There is scarcely a sentiment or an action worthy of mention which does not leave a clear trace in the budget of receipts or that of expenses'. There was more to this than mere number-crunching. Le Play believed that by applying the techniques of double-entry book-keeping to the collection and analysis of family budgets, he could explore the structure and functioning of the family as well as its material circumstances. His method included a qualitiative dimension with space reserved for the collection of information on the environment, lifestyles, values and habits of families. The data so gathered provides a mine of information which is still being quarried by historians and social scientists (Arnault, 1986).

Le Play was more than the pioneer of a particular method of social inquiry; he was equally important as the exponent of a form of liberal Catholic social thinking in which respect for private property was coupled with the sanctity of the family. The family supplied the model for the state and industry to follow. For all his admiration of the English property inheritance system, Le Play was horrified by the corrosive effects on family and social values of the rampant commercialism and unbridled industrialization proceeding across the Channel. The subversion of traditional relationships based on dependency and mutual obligation by market relations based on unrestrained individualism, promoted a dangerous degree of social inequality which France should strive to avoid. For Le Play the restoration of authority, stability, and co-operation – at home, at work and in the community – were central to the regeneration of society. His family-centred approach left little scope for state action, beyond the restoration of paternal authority through the scrapping of the inheritance laws. For the rest, he looked to a religious renaissance promoted by the exemplary conduct of the upper classes who should become models of morality and support the clergy in teaching obedience to the Ten Commandments as did the English aristocracy on their estates. He opposed governmental regulation to solve labour problems arising out of the Industrial Revolution and the collapse of the guilds, and advocated instead improved co-operation to strengthen the bonds of mutuality and obligation between employers and workers. The factory, he regarded as an extension of the family, in which the master exercised an authority over its members comparable with that of the father over his children. Trade unionism seemed unnatural and a negation of the more efficient organization derived from the family group. Likewise he set his face against big cities. France, he believed, needed non-urban industrial development where workers might benefit from the benevolent paternalism of company managers and avoid the rootlessness and moral dangers of the city.

For all that, Le Play's ideas did not travel well. Le Play's ideas were barely known in Britain before the 1890s. Although he was a pronounced Anglophile, with good cross-Channel connections, his influence upon social science in Britain was negligible. A bowdlerised version, concocted by William Lucas Sargant in 1857, had introduced *Les ouvriers européens* to an English-speaking audience without any appreciable impact upon methods of social inquiry. The reasons are not far to seek. Notwithstanding his admiration of English social and political arrangements, the neo-Catholic framework in which his ideas were presented, his rural prejudices and preoccupations with questions of entail, all served to diminish his findings. The use of family budgets, in order to study consumption patterns and living standards, were also deemed inferior to the search for conclusions that were more readily obtainable from numerous observations reduced to statistically-sound generalities (O'Day and Englander, 1993, pp.141–2).

The reconstruction of social theory, a process that had begun in the 1870s, became urgent during the 1880s as the onset of economic depression, mass unemployment an extended franchise and social unrest exposed the deficiencies in orthodox economics. Charles Booth's path-breaking survey *Life and Labour of the People in London* should be seen in relation to the search for an economic theory that was less abstract, less deductive and rather more serviceable than that of the classical school. Booth's inquiry is generally acclaimed for the first scientific estimates of poverty. But it did more than that. It was divided into three series – Poverty, Industry and Religious Influences – concerned with social, productive and cultural relations under varying conditions.

The Booth survey addressed the Labour Question or Social Question, a subject area broader than the measurement of poverty with which Booth is customarily, and erroneously, identified. It is often suggested that Booth, as a social theorist, was primarily interested in those who were incapable of independent existence and that the rest of the community could look after itself. This is not so. Booth, like most contemporaries, possessed a highly differentiated picture of the working classes. Distinctions based on skills,

Britain

income, age, regularity of employment, consumption, religion, manners and mores etc., were applied to the location of people within particular strata. The key distinctions were between skilled and unskilled, rough and respectable, deserving and undeserving, between the practitioners of self help and mutual aid who tried to preserve an independent existence and the 'residuum' of casual workers, loafers, unemployables and ne'er-do-wells whose moral and physical degeneration threatened to pull down the self-supporting elements above them.

The prevention of such convergence supplied the impetus to a bold programme of social reform. Booth believed that special action was required to remove the very poor from the labour market and argued for coercive state action in defence of individualism. The possibility was considered that the inefficient elements of the population might be forcibly segregated into labour colonies, deprived of civil liberties and subject to stringent physical controls in order to safeguard the independent or respectable working class. His subsequent advocacy of non-contributory old age pensions, a measure designed to liberate the 'true' working class from the competition of the aged poor, was simply a less repressive aspect of the same strategy. As he himself explained: 'an endowment for old people paid out of taxation would, if the amount granted be small, have no adverse but rather a favourable influence on private accumulation, and the spirit of independence would not suffer' (Harris, 1995).

Diff –
Geml
frame

In some respects the ideas of the British, French and German social reformers were remarkably similar. All were critical of political economy. All were convinced that it was in need of revision and all hoped to furnish some of the necessary empirical data for that purpose. They also shared a common agenda in respect of comparative and historical methods of inquiry. Similarly, they were all opposed to socialism and all convinced that theoretical and social requirements could be satisfied without the wholesale transformation of property relations. Their framework of social research and the conclusions drawn from it, however, were dissimilar. The German historical economists, true to the patriarchal tradition in which they had been reared, viewed the adjustment of economic and social relations among individuals as an object of statecraft. The family-centred approach of the Le Playists seemed ill-suited to the requirements of the *Kaiserreich* and the nationalist middle classes within it. *Les ouvriers européens*, when presented to Berlin students in the 1860s, was rejected out of hand. 'We wanted to study national economy, not private households', Lujo Brentano recalled (Oberschall, 1965, p.44).

Britain

The British, too, had other priorities. The idea of the state as a moral agency capable of inestimable good never captivated the British as it did the Germans. The corporatist cast of Le Play's social catholicism elicited an equally negative response. The individualism characteristic of British social thought remained a major influence, even on advanced thinkers like Charles Booth, who continued to justify state action as a special measure to liberate the self-supporting working class.

diff

How important were Booth, the *kathedersozialisten*, and the Le Playists to the formation of social policy? On the face of it, the Le Playists were the least influential. It is sometimes argued that Le Play's importance lies in the fact that 'his view of social harmony as integral to the well organized state continues throughout the social policy debate in France' (Ashford, 1986, p.83). Perhaps so. But in his own lifetime, and in the period covered by this course, his idea of family solidarity as a justification for public action was largely ignored, partly because of his self-marginalizing opposition to the growth of representative democracy, but also because the Catholic liberalism of the Second Empire was unacceptable to the leaders of the Third Republic. The British case, by contrast, displays a clearer linkage between social research and social policy. The Life and Labour Inquiry not only enlarged the informational and statistical base of the debate on the Social Question, but also helped to identify the strategies and guiding principles of collective action. It was, though, as much a matter of people as of ideas.

Recruits to the Labour Department of the Board of Trade who had cut their teeth with the Booth Inquiry included top civil servants like Sir Hubert Llewellyn Smith (1864–1945), David Frederick Schloss (1850–1912), Clara Collet (1860–1948) and Ernest Aves (1857–1917). Indeed, Booth's remarkable success in placing his people at key points within the policy-making process was such that one contemporary likened him to the 'Permanent President of the Board of Trade' (O'Day and Englander, 1993, p.16). Booth, much more than Le Play, was in tune with the dominant ideology of social reform. His coercive schemes for segregating the unemployed from the normal labour market came to nought it is true, but in his concern with market imperfections rather than social deprivation, with the competitive needs of industry rather than the welfare rights of citizenship, Booth represented the mainstream in British social legislation before the First World War. German collectivism, as displayed in the proceedings of the Social Policy Association, was equally control-minded. The suppression of revolutionary socialism and creation of a stable environment for peaceful progress (i.e. without social transformation) certainly accorded with the strategy pursued within the *Kaiserreich*. Nevertheless, the influence of the *kathedersozialisten* upon the specific form of German social insurance remains controversial, as we shall now discover.

Social insurance in Germany and Britain

The creation of state-run schemes of social insurance in Germany, Austria, Hungary, Luxembourg, Great Britain and elsewhere at the end of the nineteenth and beginning of the twentieth centuries represented a turning point in the shifting relationship between the state and its subjects. The primacy of German social legislation in this field and its wider significance, however, will not be immediately obvious from your set book. Yet the German model of comprehensive and compulsory workers' insurance fascinated individuals and governments and was a major influence upon the spread of comparable schemes in other countries. German social insurance generated a vast specialized literature and set the agenda for the regular series of international conferences at which progress was monitored, information disseminated and ideas exchanged. Georg Zacher's *Leitfaden zur Arbeiterversicherung des Deutschen Reiches*, a publication sponsored by the Imperial Insurance Office, in 1893, appeared in German, French and English versions at the world exhibition held in Chicago. Discounted at 10 pfennig per copy, it became a best-seller with 10,000 copies sold by 1895. Contemporaries, though, were not satisfied with printed accounts. The German system was keenly studied by fact-finding delegations such as those dispatched by the Conservative government in 1887 and the Liberal government in 1908. Even the labour movement – admittedly prompted by Lloyd George – sent a delegation to satisfy its curiosity. How had it come to pass that one of the most authoritarian and reactionary of regimes had become the pioneer of the most progressive social legislation of the period?

Exercise   Read Document I.25, taken from Bismarck's speeches and conversations, in connection with the introduction of the legislation of 1881. What do they tell us about Bismarck's motives in bringing forward his welfare reforms?

Discussion   The documents highlight several considerations.

1   The fear of socialism and the need to integrate workers in the polity.

2   The apprehension associated with industrialization, population growth and concentration of proletarian hordes in vast cities outwith the bounds of the traditional authority and discipline of the country-side.

3   The deficiencies in private insurance provision.

4   A concern to project the acceptable face of the German state and display its socially-benign character in the interests of class harmony and social stability.

These concerns, however, need to be placed within the broader policy of securing landowner control over the empire. The problems of governing Germany, of reconciling its divergent class, religious, agrarian, industrial and regional interests, are discussed in Anderson (pp.110–14). For Bismarck social insurance was simply a phase of a broader strategy for the preservation of the monarchical system, one that was closely connected with the reform of fiscal policy and redistribution of tax burdens in order to strengthen Germany's economy, relieve rural communities of the costs of poor relief, weaken the financial influence of the states and diminish the political influence of the Reichstag. In short, the search for new sources of tax revenue supplied the framework for social action.

In its most graspable form, Bismarck's plans were to finance accident, old age and disablement insurance from the proceeds of a proposed tobacco monopoly. This would provide the wherewithal to create a neo-corporatist Imperial Insurance Office, funded by employers' contributions and state subsidies, in which the representatives of workers and the state might compose their differences without interference from the federated states.

Bismarck, though, was not required to make bricks from straw. Prussian from head to toe, he shared the top-down traditions of his class and the interventionist impulses that came from the support of a powerful and confident bureaucracy and a weak middle class. As Chart 1 reveals, the problems of social insurance had to some extent been prefigured in the benefit funds legislation of the 1840s and 1850s. Equally important to the formation of his ideas were the experimental welfare programmes undertaken during the Second Empire (see Chart 2). As Prussian Ambassador to France in the early 1860s he had been particularly impressed with Napoleon III's paternalism. The principle of old age pensions, and the payment of meaningful state benefits, would, he believed, help to give workers a vested interest in the state, and create a proprietorial attitude tending to foster habits of prudence, caution and restraint. 'Whoever has a pension to look forward to in his old age', he told a colleague in 1881, 'is much more contented and more easily taken care of than the man who has no prospect of any.' During the liberal 1860s, for example, he, as President-Minister of Prussia, had played with the idea of a 'social monarchy' and discussed its possibilities with Ferdinand Lassalle, the leader of the German Workers Association in order to dish the Liberals. Nothing came of it. But the need for action was made increasingly pressing by the growth of the Social Democratic Party and trade union movement.

The introduction of universal, direct and equal parliamentary suffrage into the German Empire laid the basis for the growth of a united Social Democratic Party enjoying wide support. Likewise, the right to freedom of association, even when hedged with all kinds of restrictions, made possible the development of a mass trade union movement. The socialism of the Social Democratic Party, with its demand for outright land nationalization, the militancy of strike-prone trade unions and the onset of economic crisis in 1873 shook belief in progress and gave social reform a renewed urgency. The electoral success of the Social Democrats in 1874 and 1877 made answers to the Social Question imperative. The twelve seats, won in the Reichstag elections of 1877, were in themselves nothing to lose sleep over. The party had polled half a million votes and secured less than ten per cent of the vote. The distribution of those votes, however, gave cause for the deepest concern. With its 38 per cent share of the total vote in Saxony, and with 39 per cent in Berlin and 40 per cent in Hamburg, it was clear that the Socialists were poised to become the dominant political force in urban-industrial Germany.

In the ensuing public debate several distinct approaches can be identified. Christians fearing the estrangement of workers from the churches and the decline of faith in the city sought to devise outreach facilities and workers' societies in order to arrest the drift towards atheism, republicanism and socialism. Equally important in creating a climate favourable to social reform among Germany's political and bureaucratic élites was the Social Policy Association, founded in 1872, which presented conservative and liberal versions of social justice and social stability to be secured either by a monarchical state standing above class differences or by an emancipatory social policy in which worker's self-help occupied pride of place. Whatever the strategy, the *Kathedersozialisten* were agreed that state assistance was required to promote the social and political integration of a disaffected and dangerous proletariat.

Bismarck, while not committed to any particular policy, shared the anti-socialist perspective of the reformers. Repression, though considered a most valuable tool in containing the socialist labour movement, was recognized as not enough. Attention paid to burning issues of wages, working hours, housing shortages and the like would, he believed, serve to dish the socialists, restore harmony to social classes and reconcile the mass of the workers to the existing polity. His ultimate preference for social insurance over factory and minimum wage legislation for this purpose arose out of a growing concern, following the economic crisis of 1873–5, for the maintenance of German competitiveness. The anticipated improvements in labour discipline and labour productivity consequent upon the regulation of social insurance benefits were equally compelling arguments in its favour.

It was the two assassination attempts on the life of the Emperor in the summer of 1878 that provided the pretext for the suppression of socialism. Bismarck took powers to proscribe all independent labour organizations, to suppress all socialist political and economic associations, to prohibit their meetings and ban all their publications. Renewed until 1890, the anti-socialist law accounted for the suppression of over 150 periodicals and the arrest of more than 1,500 persons.

Along with the repression came attempts to display the benevolent face of the monarchical state. Social insurance was more than a cunning attempt to check socialism and improve social control; it did address real industrial problems that were growing in intensity. The risk of accidents had grown markedly with the growing number of industrial workers and widespread use of machinery (Anderson, p.143). Apart from the special case of the railways, liability for industrial injury did not extend to mine-workers, factory workers, agricultural labourers and others who had to prove employer negligence to secure compensation under the existing law. This was by no means easy and not only on technical grounds; potential witnesses feared to be implicated or dismissed if they spoke out. Then there was anxiety that compensation given against an employer could lead to bankruptcy and unemployment, and this too served to restrain would-be litigants.

Germany's sickness provisions were, if anything, worse than those concerning accident liability. In 1880 Germany's existing sickness insurance provision excluded 95 per cent of the population. The vast majority of German workers had no cover at all. Provision for old age and disablement were negligible. The incidence of occupational diseases increased while the average age of workers in industry decreased. The sustained and rapid flow of people from the countryside to the towns – in 1907 only 42 per cent of Germans living in big cities had been born there – left Germany with an ageing rural population without families to provide for them. Elderly workers and their dependants exposed to seasonal and chronic unemployment, or forced out of work through accidents, age or incapacity, had no other recourse than the poor law. In 1885 some 3.4 per cent of the population was in receipt of poor relief. One impetus towards reform came from the desire to relieve the public burden of the poor, particularly in the rural communes, and assist in the repopulation of the countryside.

German social insurance legislation introduced measures designed to rid social welfare of the stigma of pauperism. Germany's social insurance scheme transferred to the imperial government duties previously undertaken by the local authorities; in lieu of political rights it conferred social rights on workers and encouraged the view that poverty was not a form of personal inadequacy, visited arbitrarily upon individuals and their families, that had to be accepted with resignation. Unlike traditional forms of poor relief which imposed penalties on the recipients of benefits, entailing disfranchisement and engendering feelings of degradation of the acceptance of charity, Bismarckian social insurance gave the insured party a legal right to claim relief in the event of accident, sickness and disablement, independent of any means test.

Diff –

accident

Germany's social insurance system differed from the later British system in its progressive scale of old age contributions and benefits and in the extent to which it was borne by the insured party rather than the state. The irony here is that these defining features came by default rather than design. Bismarck's proposals, it will be recalled, were for an accident and old age pension insurance financed largely by the state's contributions. These, however, fell by the wayside when the tax reform programme to which they were tied was rejected by a Reichstag opposed to further extensions of the power of the imperial bureaucracy. The scheme, acceptable to the Reichstag, which gave the world the first system of compulsory national insurance, was introduced in two stages. The legislation of 1884 dealt with insurance against sickness. All regularly employed workers henceforth paid weekly contributions, graduated according to income, into a national fund, and received weekly benefits and health care when needed. In 1889 the insurance scheme was extended to embrace old age pensions, payable at 65 years of age, and financed by further contributions.

So far the introduction of German social insurance has been presented as an expression of Bismarck's political priorities. This is in line with current historical thinking. Anderson, re-stating the conventional wisdom, describes it as 'Bismarckian legislation' (p.181). But is this right? Questions arise concerning the connection between policies and personalities. Some historians, detecting a tendency to inflate Bismarck's contribution and downplay other sources of innovation, direct our attention to different aspects of the policy process.

Exercise

Read Offprint 4. Summarize Tampke's argument and say in what ways it either modifies, confirms or denies the account given above?

Discussion

Jurgen Tampke, criticizing existing interpretations, argues that the social legislation of the 1880s was much less of a radical break with the past than is often suggested. Where others see innovation, he sees continuity arguing that Germany's social insurance laws were essentially an expression of the tradition of Prussian welfare legislation, and a fleshing out of the established miner's insurance and employer welfare schemes and the ideas of the *kathedersozialisten*. The deficiencies in the various forms of social insurance and their evident failure to check class polarization and the deepening social crisis arising therefrom, are held up as proof conclusive of the essentially derivative character of the so called 'Bismarckian legislation'.

Bismarck – responsible for all policy?

There is something in this. If nothing else Tampke forcefully reminds us that we ought to pick our words carefully. Bismarck was not the sole progenitive influence on German social insurance. No question about it, he operated within a specific paternalist tradition of state social action and was subject to powerful pressures from the bureaucracy and industry who were instrumental in the shaping and implementation of the acclaimed legislation. Still, the argument is pushed too far. Ask yourself what would have happened had there been no Iron Chancellor. Would the legislation have come about when it did or taken the same form? Surely, not.

All European states were grappling with the twin legacies of the Industrial and French Revolution over the course of the nineteenth century, but as noted previously there was no uniform or linear progression from the liberal to the welfare state. German social insurance would have looked very different had it not been part of an even more controversial fiscal reform programme for which no Reichstag majority could be found. Bismarck's patriarchal proposals were substantially amended by the Liberals and the Centre Party during the process of parliamentary debate and, in consequence, made rather more responsive to the needs of a modern industrial system than might otherwise have been the case. It is surely one of the greatest of ironies that it was in the reactionary Reich rather than in the robust democracies of Britain and France, that the legislature should have been so assertive in relation to welfare legislation. Gerhard Ritter goes further. He concludes:

> On balance the Reichstag's influence on the emergence of Germany's social insurance system was probably greater than the contribution of the House of Commons to the expansion of Britain's state welfare measures in the decade before 1914. (Ritter, 1986, pp.70–1)

German social insurance would not have come about when it did without Bismarck. But this does not mean that it is accurately described as 'Bismarck's legislation'. The social insurance of the 1880s was not what Bismarck wanted. But it was all he could get.

Exercise   Turn now to your set book. There you will find an interesting discussion on sources of change and persistence in European society in which space is reserved for social welfare reforms. Look at p.181. How does Anderson account for the variation in the introduction of state-organized social insurance in Europe?

Discussion   Broadly speaking, the author sees a connection between the character of the state and the enactment of health, accident, and unemployment insurance and provision for old age. In his view it is in those states where middle-class liberalism was weak that social betterment was most likely to be advanced. As we shall see when we come to consider the backward nature of social provision in France, and the role of women in European welfare systems, there is something in this. How much, though, remains unclear. Anderson himself points to the plurality of motives in the initiation of social insurance without, however, supplying any estimate of their relative importance. We can perhaps form a better idea if we narrow the focus, for the moment, to two very different state systems. Anderson, while noting the introduction of social insurance in authoritarian Germany and democratic Britain, has little to say about the pace of change.

Nearly twenty-five years separates the introduction of national insurance in Germany from Britain. Why? Put it another way. Why was it that the first industrial nation which, we so often learn is credited with primacy in the field of social politics, should have lagged behind its North Sea neighbour for so long? Scholars, reflecting on the problem, have identified at least six reasons to account for the delayed development of social insurance in Britain in comparison with Germany. These are:

1   the weakness of class conflict;

2   strength of liberalism;

3   the differing capabilities of the state apparatus;

4   the peculiarities of the legal system;

5   the culture of self-help;

6   the adaptability of the poor law system.

Let us consider each point in turn.

Weakness of class conflict

The British working class was, in the main, much better integrated into the polity than its German counterpart. There was no mass socialist workers' movement, comparable to that of the Social Demoncratic Party, to kick-start social policy. Reconciling the workers to the political order was certainly a consideration among British policymakers, but it was not assigned the same priority as in Germany. The British trades union movement, though powerful and growing, was labourist rather than socialist in outlook, and more industrially minded than socially aware. Browned-off with the Tories and fed up with the Liberals, as undoubtedly it was, the labour movement was not alienated from parliamentary politics. Quite the contrary. The Labour Party, established at the beginning of the twentieth century, did not seek to socialize property relations but secure the legal status of trade unions. Beyond that it tended to adopt a supporting rather than a leading role in the development of social policy. Workers, particularly artisans and craftsmen, remained wary of the intervention of the state into the status-bearing self-help institution they had created. The legitimacy of the state itself, though, was never at issue (McKibbin, 1984).

The differing political frameworks in which social reform was conceived also explains the thrust of German social insurance towards the skilled workers who, as the target group for protection against the effects of accident, sickness, invalidity and old age, might be detached from socialism and reconciled to the regime. British social policy, by contrast, was less manipulative. Its tendency was towards an expansion of the scope for self-help rather than the subversion of worker organization.

Liberalism

Liberalism played a major role in the formation of social insurance in both countries. The hostility of German liberals towards state-financed social insurance, as noted earlier, was a key factor in diluting the compulsory character of Bismarck's original proposals as much on ideological grounds as any other. Liberalism peaked earlier in Germany than in Britain where the cult of the individual was more deeply rooted. The strength of liberalism in Britain may be seen not only in the predominance of the ideology of *laissez-faire*, but in the enormous popularity of the Liberal Party among working-class electors down to 1914.

State apparatus

A related point is, as we have seen, the absence of any organizational capability to intervene effectively. Social administration based on the piecemeal enlargement of the services provided by the poor law left the British without a system that could deliver an integrated welfare programme. The Royal Commission on the Poor Laws which reported in 1909 in favour of the rationalization of social service administration, merely stated publicly what the experts had long been saying privately. But by the outbreak of war nothing had been done.

Legal system

The Germans, too, were not constrained by the influence of the English Common Law with its emphasis upon private property and the law of contract. Unlike France and Germany, law in England was not viewed as the embodiment of a set of logical principles and ideas, arrived at deductively and systematically in a spirit of rationalism, but as a pragmatic art of decision by lawyers and judges based on precedent. The arrested development of public law in general left British bureaucrats without the corpus of law that served to unify and guide the activities of their counterparts in France and Germany (Lloyd, 1979, p.223).

Culture of self-help

British workers were in general more self-reliant than their German counterparts. There was nothing in Germany comparable with the network of self-creating, self-supporting and self-governing friendly societies to provide insurance against sickness, accident and other contingencies. A contribution of between 4*d* and 8*d* per week entitled the subscriber to receive sickness benefit of not more than 10*s* per week together with the free services of a doctor. Six million strong, the Friendly Societies at the beginning of the twentieth century had a membership that was five times larger than that of the trades union movement. Their strength and antagonism towards state-administered insurance schemes contributed significantly to the late development of the British social security system.

Poor law system

The revitalization of the poor law system served no less as a retardative influence upon the emergence of British social insurance legislation. In the first place, the principles of 1834 proved far more difficult to enforce than was originally envisaged so that outdoor relief, though granted on the most onerous of terms, remained more generous than that available inside the workhouse. The second, and equally significant, departure from the 'principles of 1834' came from the continuous expansion of medical services within the poor law since the middle of the nineteenth century. Medical treatment was not easily administered in conformity with the principle of less eligibility, and was, moreover, often better than that otherwise available to the poor. What, then, were the forces for change?

The introduction of the Liberal Welfare Reforms, 1906–14

It should be said, at the outset, that there is considerable disagreement among historians on the origins of the social legislation of the last Liberal government. Some have emphasized the shift in ideas and the move from Gladstonian Liberalism, as the embodiment of *laissez-faire* individualism, towards an interventionist New Liberalism, which was altogether more collectivist in character. They point to the empirical findings of Booth and Rowntree, and the encouragement their findings gave to the importance of poverty over character in the causation of social distress and the need for action to reorganize the labour market and eliminate the economically inefficient and socially harmful elements from its normal operation; they point, too, to a new awareness of the economic costs of its imperfections and of employer interest in the possibilities of social insurance to improve labour productivity, raise consumption and increase national efficiency as a solution to the problem of relative economic decline.

One school looks at the political pressures which compelled politicians to address the need for social reform; another at the basic economic and social changes from which the reforms arose. The former gives pride of place to the threat posed by Labour and the need to secure working-class votes. Others emphasize the positive contribution from a new brand of bureaucrats recruited from social scientists, economists and experts in labour relations and industrial requirements. The cadre of civil servants employed in the Labour Department of the Board of Trade (briefly encountered in our earlier discussion of Booth's ideas), have been presented as innovators whose creativity and dynamism enabled them to release British social policy from the deadening grasp of the Local Government Board and perform as key players in the policy process.

Exercise Chart 4 (Offprints Collection) outlines the salient features of the Liberal welfare reforms. There are at least three key differences between British social policy as shown here and the German scheme discussed earlier. What are they?

Discussion British social policy differed from the German in that it was fragmented, departed radically in its approach to old age pensions and was more original in respect of compulsory unemployment insurance.

The differences resist simple summary and so we shall explore them one by one.

1   The British system of non-compulsory accident insurance, was inferior to the German. The German system was not only universal in its application but was also backed by a state-enforced guarantee of payment to the worker. On the other hand cover was extended to a

wider range of occupations and, unlike German practice, also encompassed occupational diseases. Its defects received belated recognition in 1946 when it was replaced with introduction of state insurance for industrial accidents.

2   Provision for old age also differed. In contrast to Germany old age pensions in Britain were non-contributory rather than jointly financed by the employers, the insured and the state. Women claimants not in work were also eligible in Britain but not in Germany. British rates, too, were more generous than the German. On the other hand British pensions were means and character tested. The punitive spirit of the poor law is readily discerned in pensions administration. Apart from the imposition of income limits, claimants to a state pension were excluded if resident in a poorhouse and had to satisfy the authorities that they were not heavy drinkers, loafers or ex-prisoners.

3   The reservation of benefit for the deserving pensioner was typical of the social thinking represented by Charles Booth, the most persistent champion of non-contributory pensions, who saw the issue less in terms of social justice and more as an aspect of the reorganization of the labour market and creation of a more effective policy on unemployment. Pensions policy in that sense was complemented by the Labour Exchanges Act of 1909, again modelled on German experience, but departing from the German concept of municipal labour exchanges by setting up a network of public labour exchanges directly responsible to the Board of Trade.

4   British unemployment insurance was more narrow in conception than the German system being thought of primarily as a safety net to prevent the slide into destitution rather than an instrument for the maintenance of customary living standards. Hence the preference for standard rates of benefits rather than the German system of earnings-related contributions and benefits. The British system also gave much less scope for participation by the insured in the management of their affairs than the German.

However, the British system, reflecting the rather different political priorities of policymakers, gave much more scope for participation by private insurers and workers representative organizations. British legislators were not concerned to exclude trade unions from insurance administration and had no need of preferential schemes to quarantine white-collar workers. German arrangements proved more durable. The British, in trying to accommodate the approved societies, created an unworkable scheme that was replaced by a unified state administrative system in 1946.

The key problem, though, remains to account for the Liberal conversion to social insurance. Can we explain it by reference to the influence of that current of thought inspired by Hegel and the idealists of Germany, which assigned a more positive role to state action, combined with concerns for 'National Efficiency' and the feared alternative of a state social policy financed from the proceeds of protectionism? The short answer is yes but not entirely. Other considerations were just as important. A vote-winning social security programme had to be independent of the poor law, self-financing in order to avoid unacceptable rises in direct taxation and, against a background of rising unemployment, brought forward quickly.

German experience offered not so much an off-the-peg version of social insurance, as much as a model that was adaptable to British conditions. Lloyd George, like Bismarck before him, turned to insurance as a stop-gap measure in lieu of a comprehensive welfare scheme administered by the state and paid for out of taxation.

Social politics in France

Things I did

What about France? The high level of legislative activity displayed in Chart 1 should, on the face of it, warrant a good deal of attention. It will be seen that, with respect to the organization of labour, conditions of work, welfare and social insurance the French were just as active as the Germans or the British. On paper, at any rate, their achievements look impressive – free medical assistance for the poor was enacted in 1893; pensions for miners were approved in 1894 and general accident insurance introduced in 1898; laws of 1904 and 1905 extended obligatory legal provision to children in need, the aged poor of seventy years and above and to the infirm and incurable; pensions for peasants and workers were introduced in 1910 (Anderson, p.145). The French version of state-administered social insurance was patchy both in terms of the groups encompassed and the risks covered. No provision was made for compulsory unemployment insurance (which, indeed, was not introduced in France until 1958). The same was true of accident insurance; employer liability for industrial injury, established by the law of 1898, was not linked to compulsory accident insurance until 1946.

not v. good

French legislators, then, certainly kept themselves busy finding lots of things to do. But, as you will recall from our earlier discussion of the French public health, the mere passage of legislation, without proper provision of machinery for its enforcement, amounted to no more than a gesture. French legislators, though willing to raise the most controversial forms of social protection – 50 pensions bills were introduced into the legislature between 1879 and 1910 – were slow to proceed with effective forms of intervention. The reasons are not far to seek. In a nation so dominated by peasant proprietors and independent craftsmen pressure from organized labour was bound to be weaker than in the more industrially advanced economies of Germany or Britain. Furthermore, the issues raised by social insurance were less salient in a slow-growth economy that was less exposed to the effects of cyclical unemployment than competitor states. Small businessmen and peasants, who set their face firmly against redistributive taxation for welfare purposes – proposals for progressive death duties and a progressive income tax from Leon Bourgeois in 1896 – ensured that the scope for public action was limited. The absence of a system of relief comparable with the English or German poor laws was also important. The discussions and debates provoked by the reform of the poor laws, which were central to the evolution of national insurance in Britain and Germany, were muted in France where provision for the poor was not subject to compulsory legal controls by the state.

Conclusion

Diff

Questions of gender

Social policy, whether pursued by the empirical British or collectivist Continentals, was never neutral in its character or consequences. Discrimination, though, was not only age and class specific. The special legal disabilities of women were discussed earlier in the course (Unit 1). You will also recall how sex-specific roles were also embodied in the legislation and policing of prostitution. If you don't, refresh your memory and re-read the section in Unit 4 ('Legitimate force and gender'), before proceeding. It will be seen that France, Italy and (until 1886) Britain all established regulatory regimes which were offensive to middle-class women and a source of oppression to those of a lower station. In France, for example, the virtual nonexistence of women under the law made the working-class *Parisienne* liable to arrest and detention by the 'morals police' (Harsin, 1985). The methods employed in post-Risorgimento Italy were not dissimilar. Prostitutes were required to register with the police, submit to twice weekly vaginal examinations, and enter a hospital if diagnosed with venereal disease. The law also specified where they could live, when they could leave their brothels, where they could walk and what they could wear. Police permission was required to change brothels, relocate to a new city, or even be absent from their residence for more than three days (Gibson, 1986). The British regime, confined to garrison towns and seaports, displayed the same dual standard that women who became prostitutes were criminal but not the men who used them, and the same belief that prostitution was a necessary evil that ought to be controlled by the state to safeguard public health, public order and public morality.

In welfare reform, as in moral reform, there was no neutrality. Hazell Mills, in conversation with Clive Emsley (see Video 1) has some trenchant observations on the gender bias of bourgeois liberalism and the general reduction of women to their reproductive functions. You will have also noted in Chart 1 how social policies were influenced by normative assumptions about gendered roles, particularly in respect of the sexual division of labour and of social responsibility, with their in-built notions of female dependency and male earning power. Take the British Mines Act of 1842 and the French labour legislation of 1892. In both cases campaigns for limiting legislation were led by men and served to reduce female competition in the labour market, strengthen the family wage and keep women in the home. Or look at education. The French law of 1833, for example, applied only to boys; thirty-four years passed before legislation was enacted which required every commune of 500 people to provide a girl's school. The male-bias of German social insurance legislation was no less pronounced. The health insurance law of 1883 included modest maternity benefits for female factory workers as an optional extra with the implication that childbirth was a form of sickness!

The social science on which welfare legislation sometimes rested was equally partial. The Booth survey, though it gave scope to the remarkable investigative skills of Clara Collet and Beatrice Webb, paid insufficient attention to the distribution of resources within the family. In Germany, the male-dominated Social Policy Association and the equally male-centred *enquête* tradition of inquiry left little space for any meaningful expression of the opinions and interests of working women.

Exercise Does all this mean that women were a negligible influence upon the emergent welfare states? What does Anderson think? Look at his discussion of the status of women in European society (pp.175–8). In a sentence or two summarize his conclusions.

Discussion Anderson, I would say, thinks that women performed a minimal role in the creation of the European welfare state system. His account is unduly restrictive in its emphasis upon the primacy of the suffrage and overwhelmed by the marginal position occupied by women in public life. His case is, on the face of it, incontrovertible. It is undoubtedly true that women in western Europe were denied full citizenship rights. Women were excluded from the parliamentary franchise until after the First World War in Britain and Germany and denied the vote until after the Second World War in France and Italy. His account emphasizes the divisive effect of class cleavage on the feminist movement. Issues such as access to higher education and the professions or the extension of married womens' property rights, he tells us, were either an irrelevance or an affront to working-class women.

Religion was no less debilitating. Catholicism mobilized women around a satisfying alternative culture that took them out of the home but not into the public sphere. Feminism, we learn, flourished in a Protestant individualist environment like Britain. But as we shall see historians are by no means agreed on the relative importance of the Protestant ethic or the peculiarities of the polity.

Exercise Read now Offprint 5 and compare the authors' assessment with our previous, and rather gloomy, remarks. What are their findings and how do they explain them?

Discussion Koven and Michel's argument clearly attaches a much greater significance to questions of gender and women's social action in the formation of social policy. Their interpretation is not only at variance with the received wisdom as presented in Anderson's text, but also has wider implications for the account as it has unfolded so far. Their argument may be summarized thus:

1 Gender issues were a very considerable influence upon the shaping of welfare policies and programmes in the late nineteenth and early twentieth centuries. It follows that our views on the comparative importance of industrialization, social class, bureaucracy and employer participation in the genesis of the welfare state, will have to be revised.

2 It is also claimed that women exerted a substantial influence on the development of welfare states through 'maternalist politics', exercised principally through voluntary organizations. (Maternalism, it should be said, is an ambiguous term which scholars sometimes use as a shorthand for a desire to improve the position of mothers and children and sometimes as a strategy, pursued by women activists, to

extend domestic ideals into public life in order to secure female betterment and promote female solidarity.) Koven and Michel define
maternalism as 'competing ideologies and discourses that exalted
women's capacity to mother and applied to society as a whole the
values they attached to that role: care, nurturance and morality'.

3   It is further suggested that women's influence in the forty-year period
     between 1880 and 1920 was stronger in 'weak' states such as the
     United States and Britain than in 'strong' states such as Germany or
     France where the bureaucratic organization of public life left much
     less scope for women's social action.

4   In terms of agency or women's action, they argue that American
     women during the Progressive period constructed 'a kind of shadow
     welfare state' and that women's voluntary action was scarcely less
     important in Britain.

What are we to make of these claims? If they are compared with the text-
book account we might reasonably conclude that the respective authors
have:

1   read different sources or misread the same sources;

2   been on the booze;

3   inhabit different planets.

Whereas one sees women's contribution as insignificant the others find it of
enormous importance; one believes that variations in women's activism are
primarily due to the divisive effects of social class and the limiting
influence of religion, the others claim that maternalism crossed social
bridges and assert the primacy of specific state forms in determining the
space available for women's action.

   Neither account is entirely right and neither is entirely wrong. The
women's movement *was* weak, working-class women *were* under-
represented within it and its achievements *were* limited. Women in Britain,
for example, played no role in the introduction of old age pensions or in
the formulation of national health and unemployment insurance; their
influence upon protective legislation in France was also slight. Whether
this can be explained in terms of religion is debatable. But there are also
difficulties with the Koven–Michel thesis. In the first place, how are we to
characterize state structures? What is the measure of strength and weakness? As we saw earlier, states have differing capabilities dependent in no
small part upon the traditions and character of their bureaucracies. British officialdom, for example, though smaller and less interventionist than
its continental counterparts, cannot in any meaningful sense be described
as 'weak'. For all its oddities, it was not wanting in direction or purpose.
The balance of power and responsibilities between central and local
government, and the integration of public and voluntary spheres of action,
came by design rather than by default. The territory available to women in
this system was situated in voluntary action and in local government. Their
achievements within this sector are itemized in Chart 1. The point to grasp,

though, is that the frontier into the making and implementation of policy remained closed.

Paradoxically, women seem to have fared better in 'strong' states, where concerns for racial betterment, declining birth rates, high infant mortality and in the maintenance of imperial and military power, often resulted in improved maternal welfare provision. Thus French mothers secured better crèche provision and maternity leave than either British or American women. Koven and Michel tell us that this does not imply an inverse relationship between social action and social welfare, but it does leave us searching for a more useful basis for comparison.

Conclusion

The transition from the liberal to the welfare state supplies one of the key themes of modern historical inquiry. The extent to which this great transformation is a market-led development and the extent to which it embodies social values rather than capitalist priorities, has been much debated. Anderson (p.144), for example, tells us, with reference to British factory legislation, that the main inspiration was humanitarian rather than economic. Elsewhere, too, he writes of a growing desire to make life less harsh as a motive force of social reforms (Anderson, p.181). But, as we have seen, other influences might be just as important – for example the French concern with education and state-building or the German with class control. The widening of the debate in recent years to include gender issues and reinstate the role of agency has served to refine the questions without providing definitive answers. Hazell Mills, for example, has reminded us (Video 1) that French women were in some cases able to devise family strategies to overcome the restrictive provisions of the legal code with respect to married women's property rights. She does, however, agree that research in this area is still in its infancy. It is of course possible that we are barking up the wrong tree and ought to concentrate less on motives and more on means, more on the specific historical, organizational and political constraints on social action and the methods adopted to overcome them. The comparative approach enables us to do both. We have seen the growth of social legislation as a continuous, if uneven, development during the period covered by this course. We have seen, too, that states varied both in the definition of social goals and social objectives and in the capabilities and resources available for their attainment. The ideas that the expansion of social assistance and social protection was the inevitable consequence of industrialization, or that the welfare state is simply the product of market-forces, are too general to explain the specific forms of state action or assess the contribution they made to the process of state building. Circumstances matter.

References

Arnault, F. (1986), 'Histoire de F. Le Play. De la metallurgie à la science sociale', unpublished doctoral thesis, University of Nantes.

Ashford, D.E. (1986), *The Emergence of the Welfare States*, Basil Blackwell, Oxford.

Bock, G. and Thane, P. (eds) (1991), *Maternity and Gender Politics: Women and the Rise of the European Welfare States, 1880s–1950s*, Routledge, London.

Bullock, N. and Read, J. (1985), *The Movement for Housing Reform in Germany and France 1840–1914*, Cambridge University Press, Cambridge.

Englander, D. (1983), *Landlord and Tenant in Urban Britain, 1838–1918*, Oxford University Press, Oxford.

Englander, D. (1994), 'Tommy in France, 1914–1918', *Cahiers de l'Association du Souvenir de la Bataille de Verdun*, 21, pp.89–101.

Gibson, M. (1986), *Prostitution and the State in Italy, 1860–1915*, New Brunswick, New Jersey.

Harris, J. (1995), 'Civic virtue and social Darwinism: The concept of the Residuum', in D. Englander and R. O'Day (eds), *Retrieved Riches: Social Investigation in Britain, 1850–1914*, Scolar Press, London.

Harsin, J. (1985), *Policing Prostitution in Nineteenth-Century Paris*, Princeton University Press, New Jersey.

Hennock, E.P. (1987), *British Social Reform and German Precedents. The Case of Social Insurance 1880–1914*, Clarendon Press, Oxford.

La Berge, A.F. (1992), *Mission and Method: The Early Nineteenth-Century French Public Health Movement*, Cambridge University Press, Cambridge.

Lloyd, D. (1979), *The Idea of Law*, Penguin, Harmondsworth.

Marshall, T.H. (1950), *Citizenship and Social Class*, Cambridge University Press, Cambridge.

McKibbin, R. (1984), 'Why was there no Marxism in Great Britain?', *English Historical Review*, 99, pp.197–231.

O'Day, R. and Englander, D. (1993), *Mr Charles Booth's Inquiry, Life and Labour of the People in London Reconsidered*, Hambledon Press, London.

Oberschall A. (1965), *Empirical Social Research in Germany, 1848–1914*, Mouton, Paris.

Rimlinger, G.V. (1971), *Welfare Policy and Industrialization in Europe, America and Scotland*, John Wiley, New York.

Ritter, G. A. (1986), *Social Welfare in Germany and Britain: Origins and Development*, Berg Books, Leamington Spa and New York.

Weber, E. (1979), *Peasants into Frenchmen: The Modernization of Rural France, 1870–1914*, Chatto & Windus, London.

Index

Pg 144-45 - fact. acts - Brit/france
Pg 155 - Growth of cities.
Pg 157 - why not enough done,
Pg 158 - france first, then Brit
Pg 163 - emergence of attention to social questions
Pg 165 - Brit slow.